THIRSTING

TERRY FULLAM

OLIVER
NELSON

A Division of Thomas Nelson Publishers
Nashville

Published in Nashville, Tennessee, by Oliver-Nelson Books, a division of Thomas Nelson, Inc., Publishers, and distributed in Canada by Lawson Falle, Ltd., Cambridge, Ontario.

Scripture quotations are from THE NEW KING JAMES VERSION. Copyright © 1979, 1980, 1982, Thomas Nelson, Inc., Publishers.

Scripture quotation noted J. B. Phillips is from J. B. Phillips: THE NEW TESTAMENT IN MODERN ENGLISH, Revised Edition. © J. B. Phillips 1958, 1960, 1972. Used by permission of Macmillan Publishing Co., Inc.

Prayers and creeds are from *The Book of Common Prayer*, Copyright Church Pension Fund.

Printed in the United States of America.

Library of Congress Cataloging-in-Publication Data

Fullam, Terry L.
    Thirsting / Terry Fullam.
      p.   cm.
    ISBN 0-8407-9565-3
    1. Christian life—1960–   2. Bible—Criticism, interpretation,
etc. I. Title.
    BV4501.2.F84   1989
    233—dc20   89–38787
                                             CIP

1 2 3 4 5 6 — 94 93 92 91 90 89

To
the people of St. Paul's Episcopal Church,
Darien, Connecticut,
whose continual thirst for God over the years
has led us to walk together
in asking questions and seeking answers
from the One who said,
"I am the Way, the Truth, and the Life."

Contents

Acknowledgments

This book began as a sermon series several years ago. It was a favorite of many people through our tape ministry, and we had it transcribed for study purposes. When Victor Oliver sought material for our second book together, my assistant, Lynda Barnes, suggested this series and began to edit the transcriptions. As it happened, she wound up working through this series twice—the second time to mold it to Victor's concept of "Thirsting." The research and additions that flesh out the concepts represent a tremendous sacrifice of evenings and weekends of her time and energy; my appreciation is not only extended to her but to her husband, Jim, and son, Paul, who did without her while she worked!

Ruth Malloy and Alta Jelliffe proofread both manuscripts, and Oliver-Nelson's Lila Empson did the final editing. I thank God for all of their love and perseverance.

Introduction

As the deer pants for the water brooks, so pants my soul for You,
O God. My soul thirsts for God, for the living God. When shall I
come and appear before God? (Ps. 42:1–2)

David asks this question during a particularly hard time in his life.
He was in exile in the far north of Palestine, and yearned to return to
Jerusalem, to stand in the place that he understood to be the presence
of the living God. Psalms 42 and 43 comprise a beautiful poem of his
yearning and the depth of his distress. He expresses this yearning in
terms of thirsting—as a deer thirsts for the water from the brooks
during a drought, so he longs for God. This thirst is not just for
refreshment—it is to sustain life.

David realizes that his separation from God has sapped his strength
and his confidence. He hears the question of his enemies: "Where is
your God?" and commences to argue with himself. When he focuses
on the circumstances, all looks hopeless. Then he recalls the Lord's
faithfulness, and chides himself, "Why are you cast down, O my
soul? And why are you disquieted within me? Hope in God, for I shall
yet praise Him for the help of His countenance" (42:5).

David's thirst is the thirst of all who acknowledge the existence of
God and desire to sustain a relationship with Him, to seek His presence. The Bible describes this thirst in various ways; from Genesis to
Revelation it is the story of our universal thirst for God and the means
He has provided to assuage that thirst. The writers of Scripture have
used questions asked in a variety of ways to express that thirst, as
David's did. This book examines some of those questions, and the
specific lack to which each question points. For just as with physical
thirst, our soul thirsts for different things at different times.

In the English authorized version of the Bible there are 3,294 questions. There are 2,272 questions found in the Old Testament and

1,022 in the New Testament. They deal with virtually every topic having to do with our Christian faith and life. There are questions of doctrinal importance, a thirsting for knowledge, and questions of practical importance, a thirsting for guidance. In order to understand each question, we must also understand the context in which the question was asked, as well as who was asking. We will soon discover that in Scripture, questions are raised in all kinds of circumstances by all kinds of people. There are questions from saints and from sinners; those asked by God and by Jesus; by rulers and slaves; by Romans and Jews. I have chosen only a few for us to study, those that point to the soul thirst of us all. I hope they will stimulate your mind to further exploration, motivate your will to live in closer harmony with the answers, warm your heart with the experience of the love of the One who inspired them, and quench your thirst for the presence of the living God.

CHAPTER 1

Thirsting for Righteousness

THE BOOK OF JOB is regarded by some as the oldest of the writings of Scripture. It gives a wonderful glimpse into our human self-image; we instinctively know there is something fundamentally wrong with us! All the religions of the world acknowledge this fact. In the Judeo-Christian tradition, this human dysfunctionality is referred to as "sin."

This small three-letter word has been out of vogue in ecclesiastical circles for the past decade or so. The trend has been toward relativism—the lack of absolutes, and the call to accept other beliefs, giving them equal credibility with Christianity. Yet there is a universal recognition that something separates us from our God. No matter how our God may be perceived, we want to be in a right relationship with that God. There is a universal thirst for righteousness. The book of Job gives graphic examples of many of the thought patterns that express this thirst.

We are introduced to Job, a prosperous, godly father seemingly unspoiled by his prosperity. The scene quickly shifts to the throne room of the universe, where Satan insinuates that Job serves God only because of the good life he enjoys. Satan is given permission to test Job, and there follows a long narrative of Job's loss of property, family, and health. To make matters worse, Job is harangued by his wife and friends, who insist that they have the insight into what is going wrong in Job's life. Job endures much judgment and accusation from the mouths of those closest to him, who insist that his afflictions are due to unrepented sin. Job spends twenty-seven chapters defending himself and God, often questioning his friends in return.

In the fourth chapter of Job, a question is asked by Eliphaz, the most sympathetic of Job's friends. He appeals to his age and experience to lend authority to his words. He speaks of the ministry Job has had to others, saying, "Your words have upheld him who was stumbling, and you have strengthened the feeble knees; . . . Is not your reverence your confidence? And the integrity of your ways your hope?" (vv. 4, 6) Reminding Job of his own words, he goes on to share with Job a word from the Lord that he has received in a night vision, one that he is sure will bring Job to realize his sinful state. "Can a mortal be more righteous than God? Can a man be more pure than his Maker?" (v. 17). Eliphaz assumes that the answer to the question is a resounding "No."

His question is one all persons must deal with if they seek to establish a relationship with a being beyond themselves. All religions have methods to reestablish the harmonic relationship desired by all of humanity. The universal thirst for righteousness has made us seek all sorts of ways to tap into the well. The trouble is, if the pipes mankind has devised lead nowhere, all our efforts are worthless.

Scripture tells us that sin is omnipresent—both the Old and the New Testaments make that point. In Psalm 14:2–3 we read: "The LORD looks down from heaven upon the children of men, to see if there are any who understand, who seek God. They have all turned aside, they have together become corrupt; there is none who does good, no, not one."

You may be inclined to think that "there is none who does good" is an exaggeration. You could bring to mind many who do good deeds today and recall others throughout history. Using humanity as your standard of measure, you will find some who are better than others. Montaigne said that we estimate vices and weigh sins not according to *their* nature, but according to *our* advantage and self-interest. The question asked of Job is using a different standard altogether. The question is not "Can one person be more righteous than another?" but *"Can a mortal be more righteous than God?"* God Himself is the standard, and against that, none can measure up. David realized that and wrote that when God looks down upon us, He finds that we don't (or won't) understand, because we won't (or don't) seek Him, and have turned aside. David's conclusion was that we are **all** sinners. "There is none who does good, no, not one."

The God who is revealed in Scripture is holy. In Genesis 17 God reveals Himself to Abraham by saying, "I am Almighty God; walk before Me and be blameless" (v. 1). In the giving of the law, again and again, God says, "I am Holy." Hannah, the mother of Samuel, recognized this and, when worshiping, said: "No one is holy like the LORD" (1 Sam. 2:2). David asserted in another psalm: "As for God, His way is perfect" (Ps. 18:30). Through Isaiah God spoke and said: "I, the LORD, speak righteousness, I declare things that are right" (Isa. 45:19). Jesus gave us a standard of measure when He said, "Therefore you shall be perfect, just as your Father in heaven is perfect" (Matt. 5:48). He also concluded, "No one is good, but One, that is, God" (Matt. 19:17). God's holiness is one of His attributes with which the first part of Eliphaz's question deals—"Can a mortal be more righteous than God?" The answer is a resounding "NO."

Separation

The second part of Eliphaz's question asks, "Can a man be more pure than his Maker?" (see 4:17). It looks at the question from our side. One answer to the question is found in the book of Isaiah: "But your inquiries have separated you from your God; and your sins have hidden His face from you, so that He will not hear"(59:2).

The consequence of our sin is separation from God. The relationship He sought to establish by creating us in His image has been broken. It is as if a soundproof wall has been erected between us, which we cannot penetrate, break down, or overcome, "so that He will not hear." Our communications link with God is broken. How did it get that way?

What was the consequence of humanity's first sin in the Garden of Eden? When Adam and Eve disobeyed, something happened to them: they became fearful. They immediately sought to hide themselves from God. Of course it was a foolish thing to do; God knew where they were and what they had done. That is a graphic example of the way people have, throughout the ages, deluded themselves in regard to God. We pretend that we can run, we can hide, we can escape having to deal with our sins. We build our walls a little higher, so we feel somehow safer inside the confines of our sinful selves. Yet Jesus says we are to be perfect, even as our Father is perfect. We are to be holy.

Holiness has gone out of style. As people seek what they think is a more comfortable, easier way of life, holiness has become something to be admired but not desired. So we don't communicate much with God; we somehow know that in order to do so we would have to deal with the reality of our sin. What happens then? We become fearful. Sin breeds fear. Adam, who had known intimate fellowship with God, was suddenly afraid of the One who had been the very source of his life.

The very first question in the Bible is to Adam—"Where are you?" (see Gen. 3:9). It wasn't asked because God didn't know where Adam was, but because Adam didn't know he was lost, and God was trying to point that out to him!

"Where are you?" is a question that echoes through the ages. Today we ask each other a different question—"Where are you coming from?" "Where are you?" is question of confrontation—where are you now? What is going on in your heart, your mind? God continually invites us to deal with our relationship with Him. "Where are you coming from?" is a question of evasion and justification. It says, "Let's look at the past, see if we can understand what the reasons are for your actions and opinions, so we don't have to challenge you to change." Evasion is taking the long way around the problem. God loves us enough to confront us, to cut cleanly and clearly through to the heart of the problem. He says, "Where are you?"

We are all in the same place as Adam was, trying to avoid God. We are all unable to walk with God as intimately as He would desire. It is a universal condition. Paul sums it up in Romans: "for all have sinned and fall short of the glory of God" (3:23). People instinctively realize this problem; throughout the ages, all over the world they have developed some means toward overcoming it. It's called *religion*, defined as a "bond between man and the gods."

Religion

Religion is a human creation. The Latin word *religio* from which it comes originally meant "reverence for the gods." A religion has several aspects—or dimensions—concerning its beliefs, its practices, and the way it affects the individual and the society in which it exists.

One aspect of a religion is its *doctrine*. Doctrine is the belief system that gives a total explanation of reality. Another aspect is *myth,* not to be confused with fiction! Myth refers to stories about the interaction between men and their gods; myth includes stories about creation, history, salvation—examples, like Job, that people can recall, identify with, and follow. The action aspect of religion is *ethics,* the values and codes of behavior that are prescribed. Yet another aspect is *ritual;* each religion has rites of worship, festivals, initiations, rites of passage, and customs regarding food and dress. These elements make up *experience*—the individual's own sense of belonging and commitment to something outside the self. These are all seen by outsiders as the *social* aspect of religion, the way people practice their religion together and impact the world around them.

Religion is the response of human beings to the human thirst for righteousness. It is the pipe system they have devised to tap into the well. It is the effort of people to scale the wall of separation between God and themselves.

But religion is not able to quench the thirst for righteousness, no matter how faithfully it is practiced. Religion provides no more for us spiritually than a sweetened soft drink provides physically; it is able to make us feel temporarily less thirsty, but it makes no real contribution toward our well-being. Like soft drinks, there are many religions to choose from, depending on the area we live in and our preference. Some people who grew up in the 60s and 70s have shopped around, going from religion to religion as if tasting various flavors and then tiring of them, before finding the thirst-quenching love of Jesus.

Let's look at the main religions of the world, and see how they have established various formulas in order to make the believer feel righteous for a time.

Religions

In the Eastern tradition, we have Buddhism, Hinduism, and their offshoots. These are the so-called "mystical" religions, placing their emphasis on finding God within the human spirit. They deny the world and seek release from reality in the spiritual realm, through an endless round of reincarnation to which the spirit of the believer is subjected in this world.

Buddhists believe their doctrine is a vehicle (like a car or plane) that carries them across the world of suffering to their beyond. In order to attain Nirvana (complete union with perfection) they must walk the noble eightfold path of eight "right steps": Right views, right intentions, right speech, right action, right livelihood, right effort, right concentration, and right mindfulness. In order to do that, they must hold to the four noble truths: the truth of suffering, of the origin of suffering; of the overcoming of suffering, and the way to overcome suffering. They must also live moral lives based on five precepts: refraining from injury to living things, refraining from stealing, refraining from sexual immorality, avoiding falsehood, and avoiding the use

of alcohol and drugs. If they want to advance, they are asked addition-
ally to abstain from things like eating after noon, dancing, singing and
amusement, and the use of cosmetics or other adornment. If you are a
Buddhist monk, in addition to all this, you don't sleep in a comfortable bed or take money from anyone.

If you were *Hindu,* you would be bound by your birth; the caste
into which you were born would govern the progress you could make
in the next life, based on countless observations and rituals. If you
were not born in a good caste this time around, well, better luck next
time!

Hinduism has almost as many versions as there are villages or
groups of Hindus. There are hundreds of variations and even more
hundreds of gods—enough for each believer to have his or her own
personal god. Hindus believe in one high god—Brahman, "the absolute," who rules with these many lesser gods. There are three main
Hindu sects—seen as three main ways of viewing their "Brahman."
One sect believes in Vishnu, in one of his ten incarnations. Vishnu is
believed to be full of good will toward the believer, and sits enthroned
with his wife, except for those times he becomes human out of concern for the world. A second sect believes in Shiva, who is dark and
grim, and lurks in battlefields, and cemeteries. He is seen either dancing as he destroys the world or in creative meditation. There is animal
sacrifice involved in his worship, and his followers inflict pain upon
themselves. The third sect is devoted to the great Mother Goddess,
Shakti. In this point of view the god in his male aspect is not active
and does not need worship.

Regardless of their sects, the Hindus practice a way of life, a path
of duty to be followed within a strictly ordered society. There are four
great castes—or classes—then there are the outcasts and unclassified
people. Each caste has its appropriate duty. Each, in fact, is looked
upon as a totally separate species. There is no understanding of common humanity here—you are either a priest, a noble, a merchant or
peasant, a worker, or a nothing! You are forbidden to associate with a
person of another caste. This separation is strictly observed in Hindu
cultures, because the path of duty is the way of salvation; faithful
observance obtains the release of the soul from the continuous cycle
of life, death, and rebirth.

The so-called "Western Religions" are considered to be Judaism,
Christianity, Islam, and their offshoots. Western thought is based on
revelation—One God has revealed Himself to humanity from *outside*

the human spirit. Belief in a God who has revealed Himself is world-affirming rather than world-denying, stemming from belief in a Creator, and acknowledging the need of redemption in relation to Him.

The Judeo-Christian beliefs are united to a point, but the belief of Islam is separated from that of Judaism and Christianity. Why? Because salvation in Islam depends wholly upon the actions of its believers, much as in Eastern religions.

Islam has five pillars that every believer must embrace: the confession of faith, prayer five times daily facing Mecca; fasting during the month of Ramadan—no food or drink, smoking, or other carnal pleasures (though most fast during daylight hours and feast after sundown), giving an absolute 2.5 percent of their income to charity, and making a pilgrimage to Mecca once in their lives. Islam is a religion of submission—the word *Islam* comes from a root meaning "surrender." Islam seeks to conquer the world. Muslims believe that Islam meets all mankind's spiritual needs through the Koran (Qur'an), their "absolutely infallible" word of Allah, which (whether it is understood or not) brings grace through its recitation; combined with the Hadith, or tradition. These form Islamic law, which is a comprehensive guide to life and conduct. In other words, what Moslems do or don't do determines the outcome of their lives.

Jews hold certain things to be essential to faith, all of which have been continued in Christianity. These essentials are: the existence of the Creator, His unity, His spiritual nature, His eternity, His unchanging nature, His omniscience, an obligation to serve and worship Him, the validity of prophecy, the revelation of His will, the fact of retribution in this world and the next, the resurrection of the dead, and the coming of the Messiah. Sadly, even God's chosen people had broken down the beautiful relationship that was offered them into thousands of small rituals and laws governing every move they made.

Christians understand Jesus to be the Messiah, the completion and definition of the law and the prophets, who came in the flesh and will come again. The early Christian creeds teach the deity of Christ and the living, continuing presence of the Holy Spirit, who, with the Father, comprise the Holy Trinity. Christians believe that Jesus' death on the cross has atoned for our sins and that His resurrection has opened the way to the Father. We understand this by faith, and accept the written Word of God, the Bible, to be our ultimate authority in life. Yet Christianity has separated itself into thousands of denominations, each holding to one particular facet of faith above another, and developing rules, regulations, and rituals to go with them. It seems we humans will spare no amount of effort to overcome the separation of sin, but we are not willing to face it and to deal with it, to confess it and to be cleansed from it!

In many ways over the centuries, Christians have reduced Christianity to religious acts. But friends, understand this—Christianity is *not* a religion! That may come as a surprise to you, because the world does not understand Christianity. Religion is a human attempt to reconcile with God, and Jesus Christ came to make it clear that task was impossible! There is no way that any rule or ritual will reunite the Creator with His creation. Yet the notion of a salvation of works is so entrenched in the heart of humanity that it is almost impossible to dislodge. You might ask a Christian if he or she is a Christian and receive the response, "Well, I hope so; I'm trying!" Some believe they are more righteous than others because they pray more, or attend church more often, or give more of their time and money to the church and charities. They feel there are various "brownie points" God should note. But if that is the basis on which Christians seek to satisfy their thirst for righteousness, they will never be satisfied.

Fig Leaves and the Shedding of Blood

Let's go back to Adam and Eve once again. When they sinned, what did they do? They hid! Scripture says they knew they were naked, and they were ashamed. What a profoundly simple statement! Adam and Eve, representing both varieties of humanity, male and female, realized they were stripped of the righteousness they had from God and they became "self-conscious." They became aware of themselves, their condition, *our* condition. They became aware that something was missing that was a part of their relationship with God. Prior to that time, they had been able to walk with God, talk with God, and stand before Him just as they were. Now they were ashamed of who and what they were and what they had done, so they hid themselves. They took fig leaves, sewed them together, and made little aprons to cover their physical nakedness (see Gen. 3:7). The sewing of fig leaves was the first religious act of humanity.

All the religions of the world are garments of fig leaves. As time has passed, the endless creativity of humanity has designed varying styles of fig leaves, even some complex varieties. But they are all pitiful efforts to somehow make us think we look right with God when we know we do not. The acts of religion cover our shame and hide our guilt, or at least divert the attention of others from it as they watch us perform them. Whether performed in the deepest jungles of the East or the grandest cathedral of the West, religious acts are nothing more than fig leaves.

God, of course, rejected this covering. Instead, God took an animal and skinned it to provide a covering for Adam and Eve (see Gen. 3:21). Blood was shed—the animal had to die for its skin to be taken—in order to provide the covering. At the very beginning of history, God established the fact that innocent blood must be shed in order to cover sin.

God revealed to His people, Israel, a whole system whereby they could approach Him to overcome this universal sense of sin. The plan of God is so beautiful, so tender, so loving, that I think it can best be portrayed by drawing you a word picture.

Leviticus 16 is God's "show and tell," where He does something vividly and graphically before the people of Israel to show them what is necessary to become righteous in His sight. It is the description of the Jewish ritual of the Day of Atonement, Yom Kippur.

Verse 5 speaks of the actions of the high priest: "And he shall take from the congregation of the children of Israel two kids of the goats as a sin offering, and one ram as a burnt offering." We are concerned here with the sin offering—what does God do with the sin of man? Verse 7: "He shall take the two goats and present them before the LORD at the door of the tabernacle of meeting."

The tabernacle was the tent in the wilderness, with the twelve tribes of Israel camped round about it, three on each side. Aaron, the high priest, took the two goats, and put them before the door of the tabernacle in full view of all of the tribes of Israel. Verse 8: "Then Aaron shall cast lots for the two goats: one lot for the LORD and the other lot for the scapegoat."

The lots that were cast were perhaps just two pieces of pottery shards, the larger of which would be for the Lord. Today we might say "Heads for the Lord, tails for the scapegoat" and flip a coin. When the lots were cast, one goat became "for the LORD." Verse 9: "And Aaron shall bring the goat on which the LORD's lot fell, and offer it as a sin offering."

The goat on which the Lord's lot fell was killed and offered as a sacrifice. Verse 10: "But the goat on which the lot fell to be the scapegoat shall be presented alive before the LORD, to make atonement upon it, and to let it go as the scapegoat into the wilderness."

A goat was killed and another was presented alive before the Lord. An animal had to lose his life in order to provide atonement for the sins of the people, just as one had to die in the Garden of Eden to provide a covering. To make humanity presentable before God required the death of an innocent victim.

> And when he has made an end of atoning for the Holy Place, the tabernacle of meeting, and the altar, he shall bring the live goat; and Aaron shall lay both his hands on the head of the live goat, confess over it all the iniquities of the children of Israel, and all their transgressions, concerning all their sins, putting them on the head of the goat, and shall send it away into the wilderness by the hand of a suitable man. The goat shall bear on itself all their iniquities to an uninhabited land; and he shall release the goat in the wilderness (Lev. 16:20–22).

Can you imagine the picture as God graphically portrayed it before the Israelites? The seriousness of their sin and separation necessitated the death of an innocent victim offered as an atonement to God. In addition, their sins were transferred to another who was sent off, taking their sins far from them. As the goat went farther from them, they knew their sins would no longer count against them.

The Lamb of God

It took two goats to tell that story to the Israelites. Seven hundred and fifty years before Christ, by the divine inspiration of the Holy Spirit, the prophet Isaiah wrote yet another word picture of the salvation of God.

> Surely He has borne our griefs
> And carried our sorrows;
> Yet we esteemed Him stricken,
> Smitten by God, and afflicted.
> But He was wounded for our transgressions,
> He was bruised for our iniquities;
> The chastisement for our peace was upon Him,
> And by His stripes we are healed.
> All we like sheep have gone astray;
> We have turned, every one, to his own way;
> And the LORD has laid on Him the iniquity of
> us all (Isa. 53:4–6).

Isaiah was shown the true meaning of the levitical sacrifice over the centuries: "And Aaron shall bring the goat on which *the Lord's lot fell,* and offer it as a sin offering" (Lev. 16:9, *italics mine*). The Bible makes it clear that the blood of goats and lambs could never take away sin. When the scapegoat left, it was to portray the concept of what God was going to do. Isaiah saw through the inspiration of the Holy Spirit that what God was going to do was to take our sin upon Himself—the scapegoat—and sacrifice His own blood in an atoning act for those sins. This was the "lot" of the Lord Jesus Christ.

No doubt you will recall the words of John, the baptizer, when he first saw Jesus on the banks of the Jordan: "Behold! The Lamb of God who takes away the sin of the world" (see John 1:29). Peter wrote in his first letter:

> And if you call on the Father, who without partiality judges according to each one's work, conduct yourselves throughout the time of your stay here in fear; knowing that you were not redeemed with corruptible things, like silver or gold, from your aimless conduct received by tradition from your fathers, but with the precious blood of Christ, as a lamb without blemish and without spot (1 Peter 1:17–19).

What gained our salvation? The blood of Jesus Christ. It was His willingness to die that makes Good Friday important. Don't ever think that on Good Friday you observe the untimely death of a martyr to some lost cause. Good Friday marks the self-sacrifice of God Himself on our behalf. One can almost imagine that God confessed the sins of the world on His Son as He hung on the cross—that transfer that took place and gave Jesus His first taste of separation from His Father. No wonder He cried, "Why have you forsaken Me?"(see Mark 15:34).

Do you see why understanding Christians sing joyfully about the blood of Jesus? The concept is offensive to the world; the world believes that we can bridge the gap on our own strength. One skeptic referred to Christianity as "the slaughterhouse religion." Christianity is not a religion. It's a relationship with Jesus Christ. It is bloody, and the blood could not be more precious. We were ransomed, we were redeemed by the blood of the Son of God, and nothing else. We couldn't buy our way or work our way to salvation, no matter how many lifetimes we had. The work of salvation was done for us, by

Jesus, in a supreme act of love, and He seeks only to share that love and salvation with us. The righteous, innocent One died in the place of the guilty world so that the wall of separation erected by our sin might be brought down. As an illustration of that fact, the curtain in the temple was torn in two when Jesus died—there was no longer any need to separate God from His people. Why have people been trying to sew the curtain back up ever since?

Paul states the case most clearly: "For He (the Father) made Him who knew no sin (Jesus, His Son) to be sin for us, that we might become the righteousness of God in Him" (2 Cor. 5:21).

Do you remember Eliphaz's question? "Can a mortal be more righteous than God? Can a man be more pure than his Maker?" Not if he has to rely on his own acts, his own righteousness. If all one has are the fig leaves of religion, all is lost. We can't trust in the things we have done. But if we trust in the relationship we have with Jesus Christ, we have His purity, His righteousness. He assumed our part so that we could assume His. If we believe that, then the righteousness of God is credited to our bankrupt account, we stand righteous and holy with the holiness of God, and our thirsting for righteousness is no more.

Don't turn your Christianity into a morality of doing good and thinking you're being good. Don't cheat yourself of something profoundly more important. If you have given your life to Jesus Christ and accepted Him as your Savior, you are His. If not, think about this: The cross of Jesus is a symbol of God "crossing out" your sins. One day, we will all stand before God. How will you stand? Wrapped in the fig leaves of religion? Or clothed in the righteousness of Christ, perfect, restored to a relationship with God, accepted, protected, redeemed, purified, and washed in the blood of the Lamb?

PRAYER

Set us free, O God, from the bondage of our sins, and give us the liberty of that abundant life which you have made known to us in your Son our Savior Jesus Christ; who lives and reigns with you, in the unity of the Holy Spirit, one God, now and for ever. Amen.

—Collect for the Fifth Sunday after the Epiphany

— QUESTIONS —

In terms of your relationship with God, "Where are you?"

What aspects of other world religions do you find are a part of your beliefs?

What religious acts make you feel righteous for awhile?

What makes you uncomfortable when you think about being washed in the blood of Jesus?

CHAPTER 2

Thirsting for Reconciliation

SOME PEOPLE SAY the Bible is the story of humanity's quest for God. When I hear this said, I am sure that the speaker has never read the Bible with any degree of understanding or comprehension of its content. The Bible is not the story of humanity's search for God, but the story of God's progressive, continual revelation of Himself to humanity.

In the last chapter we saw that we cannot break down the barrier between ourselves and God—that any attempt to do so has to come from God's side. Well, once the barriers are down, and a relationship has been reestablished, then what? Is accepting the atoning work of Jesus Christ on the cross for us the end of all that God expects or desires from a relationship with us? Can we really imagine that God wants to stop there?

Apparently many do think that, because many come forward to receive Christ over and over and over again and never go on to the next step of the relationship, which is living with God. They are apparently still asking a question that Solomon asked, "But will God indeed dwell with men on the earth?" (2 Chron. 6:18). That question expresses both a doubt and a desire. The desire is the thirst for reconciliation—a healed relationship with God. The doubt is wondering if it really is possible that a holy God would want that. It stems from generations of a sinful self-image. Let me reassure you—this has been God's intention from the very start.

Phase I—The Tabernacle

When Moses went up on Mount Sinai, in addition to the tablets of the law, he received from the Lord building instructions for a tabernacle. The Lord designed a four-sided tent. Three tribes were to camp on each side of it, so that the twelve tribes of Israel gathered with the Lord in their midst. The instructions Moses received were extremely detailed. When the tabernacle was finished, it was wonderful to behold. Made out of skins dyed beautiful colors, it was designed so that it could be taken down easily and carried as the Israelites moved from campsite to campsite during their wilderness wanderings. At each site, the tent was to symbolize the presence of God dwelling with His people. God spoke of His purpose:

> And there I will meet with the children of Israel, and the tabernacle shall be sanctified by My glory. So I will consecrate the tabernacle of meeting and the altar. I will also consecrate both Aaron and his sons to minister to Me as priests. I will dwell among the children of Israel and will be their God. And they shall know that I am the LORD their God, who brought them up out of the land of Egypt, that I may dwell among them. I am the LORD their God (Ex. 29:43–46).

The glory of the tabernacle was the presence of God within it, not its beautiful construction. Not even the fact that the instructions were given by God made that place holy; had God not dwelt within it, it would have been just an inspired work of art. God had said, "the tabernacle shall be sanctified by My glory," and "I will dwell among the children of Israel and will be their God." He was drawing near to His people by His presence in that tent.

The tabernacle was not a place where the people gathered to worship God. The Lord's presence was there, but none could go into His presence, into the chamber known as the "Holy of Holies," except the high priest, and he could go in on only one day out of the year—on the Day of Atonement. God was present, but He was not approachable.

Read what happened at the dedication of the tabernacle when it was finished. "Then the cloud covered the tabernacle of meeting, and the glory of the LORD filled the tabernacle. And Moses was not able to enter the tabernacle of meeting, because the cloud rested above it, and the glory of the LORD filled the tabernacle" (Ex. 40:34–35).

Just as God had promised, His glory filled the tabernacle. His presence was a guide to the Israelites, and a governance to their lives.

> Whenever the cloud was taken up from above the tabernacle, the children of Israel would go onward in all their journeys. But if the cloud was not taken up, then they did not journey till the day that it

was taken up. For the cloud of the LORD was above the tabernacle by day, and fire was over it by night, in the sight of all the house of Israel, throughout all their journeys (Ex. 40:36–38).

Phase II—Solomon's Temple

In 1 Chronicles 17 we find the Israelites settled into the land of Canaan. The tent of the tabernacle had functioned for many, many years. It was given during Moses' leadership in the wilderness, and it was forty years before the Israelites finally came to the land of promise. No doubt successive tents were made according to the same instructions. When they came into the land, they brought the tent of tabernacle with them. Finally, as the nation settled into the land and consolidated under David's rule as king, he desired to build a more permanent place for the Lord to dwell among His people. David wanted to build a temple.

> Now it came to pass, when David was dwelling in his house, that David said to Nathan the prophet, "See now, I dwell in a house of cedar, but the ark of the covenant of the LORD is under tent curtains." Then Nathan said to David, "Do all that is in your heart, for God is with you." But it happened that night that the word of God came to Nathan, saying, "Go and tell My servant David, 'Thus says the LORD: "You shall not build Me a house to dwell in. For I have not dwelt in a house since the time that I brought up Israel, even to this day, but have gone from tent to tent, and from one tabernacle to another. Wherever I have moved about with all Israel, have I ever spoken a word to any of the judges of Israel, whom I commanded to shepherd My people, saying, 'Why have you not built me a house of cedar?'"' Now therefore, thus shall you say to My servant David, 'Thus says the LORD of hosts: "I took you out from the sheepfold, from following the sheep, to be ruler over My people Israel. And I have been with you wherever you have gone, and have cut off all your enemies from before you, and have made you a name like the name of the great men who are on the earth. Moreover I will appoint a place for My people Israel, and will plant them, that they may dwell in a place of their own and move no more; nor shall the sons of wickedness oppress them anymore, as previously, since the time that I commanded judges to be over My people Israel. Also I will subdue all your enemies. Furthermore, I tell you that the LORD will build you a house."'" (1 Chron. 17:1–10).

David was full of good intentions, but he was running ahead of God. God needed to remind him that, in spite of all the power and position that was seemingly his, it was God who had given them to him, and God would do the rest. I'm particularly interested in what the Lord said next to David. It is a striking prophetic word. As you read it, remember that David lived about one thousand years before Christ. This word is an example of the kind of prophetic writing that has a double interpretation. There is an immediate fulfillment and then there is a fulfillment of greater duration and extent.

> And it shall be, when your days are fulfilled, when you must go to be with your fathers, that I will set up your seed after you, who will be of your sons; and I will establish his kingdom. He shall build Me a house, and I will establish his throne forever. I will be his Father, and he shall be My son; and I will not take My mercy away from him, as I took it from him who was before you. And I will establish him in My house and in My kingdom forever; and his throne shall be established forever (1 Chron. 17:11–14).

The immediate fulfillment of the prophecy was that the Lord did raise up Solomon, one of David's sons, to succeed him on the throne of Israel. It was Solomon who built the great temple around the year 940 B.C. A record of its construction is found in 2 Chronicles 3—4.

Solomon's temple was a magnificent structure. It was made of cypress overlaid with gold, adorned with precious stones. It was legendary in its own time; people came from far and wide to view its splendor.

When the day finally came to dedicate the temple, Solomon gathered the elders of Israel and all the tribal heads for a feast. They offered sacrifices to God, and it is written:

> Indeed, it came to pass, when the trumpeters and singers were as one, to make one sound to be heard in praising and thanking the LORD, when they lifted up their voice with the trumpets and cymbals and instruments of music, and praised the Lord, saying:
> "For He is good,
>   For His mercy endures forever,"
> that the house, the house of the LORD, was filled with a cloud, so that the priests could not continue ministering because of the cloud; for the glory of the LORD filled the house of God (2 Chron. 5:13–14).

Solomon addressed the people, reciting the tale of Nathan's word to David concerning the building of the temple. Then Solomon knelt before the altar of the Lord and spread out his hands toward heaven in prayer. Acknowledging the greatness and faithfulness of God, he wondered aloud at how insignificant a work he had done for so great a God. And he asked a question: "But will God indeed dwell with men on the earth? Behold, heaven and the heaven of heavens cannot contain You. How much less this temple which I have built!" (2 Chron. 6:18–19).

Even as his part of the prophetic word was being fulfilled, Solomon knew that the worship and sacrifices at the glorious temple would not bring about the reconciliation with God for which he and his people thirsted.

The Promise

Let's look at God's promise to David again, more closely. The Lord said, "I will be his Father, and he shall be My son" (1 Chron. 17:13). That's an unusual way of speaking in the Old Testament. The writers of the Old Testament Scriptures could not have spoken of Solomon as the son of God and the Lord as his Father. God also promised David, "I will not take My mercy away from him, as I took it from him who was before you" (that is, Saul, who was king before David). God further promised to establish his son in two places—"in My house and in My kingdom forever, and his throne will be established forever."

Where was the house of the Lord? From Moses through David, it was the tent of the tabernacle. In Solomon's time, it was the temple. Yet the Son of God was going to be established in God's house, and his throne would be in God's kingdom. There is a double symbolism emerging here: the worship of God, as symbolized by the tabernacle and temple, and the Kingdom of God, as symbolized by the throne. Further illumination is found in a prophetic word in the book of Jeremiah, who wrote this about four hundred years after David, six centuries before Christ.

> "Behold, the days are coming," says the LORD,
> "That I will raise to David a Branch of righteousness;
>   A King shall reign and prosper,
>   And execute judgment and righteousness in the earth.
>   In His days Judah will be saved,
>   And Israel will dwell safely;
>   Now this is His name by which He will be called:
>   THE LORD OUR RIGHTEOUSNESS" (Jer. 23:5–6).

At the time that the prophecy was given, David had been dead for four hundred years, yet the Lord said that he was going to arise up for David a righteous Branch. The original promise made to David was to put one of his descendants upon the throne. Now God is saying, "I will raise to David a Branch of righteousness," (note that the "B" is capitalized), whose name is "THE LORD OUR RIGHTEOUSNESS." This is no ordinary son of David!

We find another striking prophecy among the writings of the prophet Zechariah, who wrote about 450 years before Christ. It is a prophecy made to Joshua:

> Behold, the Man whose name is the BRANCH!
> From His place He shall branch out,
> And He shall build the temple of the LORD;
> Yes, He shall build the temple of the LORD.
> He shall bear the glory,
> And shall sit and rule on His throne;
> So He shall be a priest on His throne,
> And the counsel of peace shall be between
> them both (Zech. 6:12–13).

Solomon's glorious temple was destroyed in the year 586 B.C. A second temple was built seventy years later, and that one stood in Jesus' day. There was a temple standing when this prophecy was given, yet it is clear that the BRANCH is yet coming, a Man who will build the temple of the Lord. Not only that, but the BRANCH was going to bear the glory that had inhabited the tabernacle and Solomon's temple and the second temple. The BRANCH was going to bear the glory that none could bear—that any mortal who encountered it had to flee. He would sit and rule on His throne, as a priest. David was promised a descendant who would build a temple, a place of worship of God, and establish a throne, symbolizing the kingdom of God. Here Zechariah is saying that the one upon the throne would also be a priest. The kingship and the worship of God would be fulfilled together in one person, the BRANCH.

The BRANCH

But while he [Joseph] thought about these things, behold, an angel of the Lord appeared to him in a dream, saying, "Joseph, son of David, do not be afraid to take to you Mary your wife, for that which is conceived in her is of the Holy Spirit. And she will bring forth a

Son, and you shall call His name JESUS, for He will save His people
from their sins." So all this was done that it might be fulfilled which
was spoken by the Lord through the prophet, saying, "Behold, the
virgin shall be with child, and bear a Son, and they shall call
His name Immanuel," which is translated, "God with us" (Matt.
1:20–23).

The BRANCH was born, and they named Him Jesus. The doctrine
of the incarnation of the Lord Jesus Christ is that God became man
and dwelt among us. Here is the answer to Solomon's question, "Will
God indeed dwell with men on the earth?" The God who was holy
and unapproachable on Mount Sinai, who lived in the tabernacle with
such glory in His presence that He could not be approached, that
same God chose to dwell among us in human form. Not only did He
choose to dwell among us, but He came with a purpose! That purpose
was to die. "Jesus answered and said to them [the Pharisees], 'Destroy this temple, and in three days I will raise it up.' Then the Jews
said, 'It has taken forty-six years to build this temple, and will You
raise it up in three days?' But He was speaking of the temple of His
body" (John 2:19–21).

Jesus was God in human flesh, and His body was a temple. He was
accessible; people crowded around him, even small children surrounded Him. God in human form was approachable. He could be
touched, seen, audibly heard. The God who had been above us became God with us, Immanuel.

Living Temples

But the prophecy to David also said that the Branch who sat upon
the throne was going to *build* a temple. What is the temple that Jesus
built? It wasn't His physical body; He inhabited that. The answer to
that question was revealed to the apostle Paul, and He speaks of it in
Ephesians.

Now, therefore, you are no longer strangers and foreigners, but fellow citizens with the saints and members of the household of God,
having been built on the foundation of the apostles and prophets,
Jesus Christ Himself being the chief cornerstone, in whom the
whole building, being fitted together, grows into a holy temple in the
Lord, in whom you are also being built together for a dwelling place
of God in the Spirit (Eph. 2:19–22).

God's plan and purpose in His Son was to unite Jew and Gentile together into one people. That people would be the temple Jesus would build, Himself being the chief cornerstone. Being joined together by the Lord, they would grow into a holy temple in the Lord, a habitation for the Spirit of God.

The temple the Branch built is the church. It is not a building of wood, stone or masonry, steel or glass. The church that Jesus builds is a living temple, made up of people who are one, no longer strangers and foreigners to one another. God has chosen to dwell in the hearts of His people; we are the habitation of the Spirit of God. Paul reinforces that thought: "Do you not know that you are the temple of God and that the Spirit of God dwells in you? If anyone defiles the temple of God, God will destroy him. For the temple of God is holy, which temple you are" (1 Cor. 3:16–17).

"Or do you not know that your body is the temple of the Holy Spirit who is in you, whom you have from God, and you are not your own? For you were bought at a price, therefore glorify God in your body and in your spirit, which are God's" (1 Cor. 6:19–20).

Jesus holds the mortgage on the temple He built. We were bought with a price. God has purchased us with the blood of His Son, and has come to dwell within us by His Holy Spirit. Do you think for a minute that the temple in which He has made such a costly investment and in which He has chosen to live is one He is going to neglect? God is not an absentee landlord! He will tend to every detail that is brought to His attention. The trouble comes when we don't bring things to His attention soon enough. Then the problem gets worse; soon the temple becomes uninhabitable. God cares about the way the temple reflects the life of its inhabitant. If the Holy Spirit dwells within us, He wants us to radiate some evidence of His presence. The glory of God was noticeable when He dwelt in tents and temples; should it be less when He dwells within us? Jesus referred to this idea when he said:

"You are the light of the world . . . Let your light so shine that people may see your good works and glorify your Father in heaven."

That is true of the individual and the corporate life of the church. We are the temples that the Messiah, the Branch, is building, and the building is always in process. There are constant "renovation" projects going on. Some repairs are minor, some cosmetic, and some require the tearing down of one area in order to build another that will be more useful to the Lord. This is how the Lord protects His investment—He constantly makes improvements!

There has been much concern expressed in the media about the decline of membership in what are known as the "mainline denominations." What has happened is that some of the more established "temples" have fallen into disrepair. They have moved away from being theologically orthodox in the sense that they accept all the teachings of the early Christian creeds. They have ceased to take the Bible as the ultimate authority for their lives. Once that important foundation has eroded, there is little to sustain the life of these denominations, and they become dangerous to inhabit. Renovation, if not reconstruction, is necessary. The churches need to be renewed and restored, to be reconciled with God.

Renewal is happening in a lot of places, but God has lots of work yet to be done. He can use all the helping hands He can find—those with hearts willing to speak His word within the structures of the mainline denominations and work within them to restore them. God has made a large investment in His churches. The reason for the decline in membership is that people have gone elsewhere to receive the message of the gospel for which they thirst. If the churches will once again become fit dwelling places for the Lord, He will inhabit them in the hearts of His people.

Paul's words to the church at Corinth are contemporary today. He speaks of the ministry of reconciliation as knowing what it is to have a relationship with the Lord, then trying to persuade others, because Christ's love compels him to do so. Then he goes on to say that we regard no one from a worldly point of view, because if anyone is in Christ, he is a new creation. Therefore, we have been given the ministry of reconciliation—God's bringing the world to Himself through Christ, not counting our sins against us. God makes His appeal to the world through His churches—and it is to them today that Paul says, "We implore you on Christ's behalf, be reconciled to God" (2 Cor. 5:20).

I've heard so much talk about the "social gospel" versus "the gospel." The social gospel is only part of the gospel story—it's not the whole counsel of God. The problem is, we can't make the social gospel work without the gospel of faith, of reconciliation, of the rule of Christ. Proclamation won't work without demonstration, either. The world won't believe the words unless they see the acts. Both, in balance—that's God's purpose.

Our Priesthood

Not only are we temples of God, but we are His priests, also. "Coming to Him as to a living stone, rejected indeed by men, but chosen by God and precious, you also, as living stones, are being built up a spiritual house, a holy priesthood, to offer up spiritual sacrifices acceptable to God through Jesus Christ" (1 Peter 2:4–5).

As the holy priesthood with Jesus as the Great High Priest, we are to offer spiritual sacrifices acceptable to God in our worship, in the lives we lead, in the thoughts we have.

What might those spiritual sacrifices be? Jesus directed us to repentance and mercy: "But go and learn what this means: "I desire mercy and not sacrifice.' For I did not come to call the righteous, but sinners, to repentance" (Matt. 9:13).

Paul thought love was important: "And walk in love, as Christ also has loved us and given Himself for us, an offering and a sacrifice to God for a sweet-smelling aroma" (Eph. 5:2).

The writer of the book of Hebrews found faith and obedience fit sacrifices: "By faith Abel offered to God a more excellent sacrifice than Cain, . . . By faith Abraham obeyed" (Heb. 11:4, 8). From that writer we also receive guidance to the spiritual atmosphere that is to pervade the temple of the Holy Spirit. It is to begin, end, and infuse all of the sacrificial acts: "Therefore by Him let us continually offer the sacrifice of praise to God, that is, the fruit of our lips, giving thanks to His name" (13:15). This is the sacrifice of praise, of gratitude for having been reconciled, rebuilt, chosen as a dwelling place of God.

Out of this sacrifice will flow the life of compassion and strength extended to others. "But do not forget to do good and to share, for with such sacrifices God is well pleased" (13:16).

Will God Dwell with Me?

In Revelation 21, Saint John says: "And I heard a loud voice from heaven saying, 'Behold, the tabernacle of God is with men, and He will dwell with them, and they shall be His people. God himself will be with them and be their God'" (21:3).

John heard all of heaven declare it: the tabernacle, the dwelling place, the temple of God is with men; He will dwell with them, if they will be His people. If they choose Him, He will dwell with them. God has come to dwell in us, among us, with us. He wants to work through us. Solomon's question is clearly answered in Scripture; the God above us became, in Jesus, God with us, and, in the Holy Spirit, God within us, that His will may be accomplished, that our thirst for reconciliation may be fulfilled.

___ PRAYER ___

Almighty God, you have built your Church upon the foundation of the apostles and the prophets, Jesus Christ himself being the chief cornerstone: Grant us so to be joined together in unity of spirit by their teaching, that we may be made a holy temple acceptable to you; through Jesus Christ our Lord, who lives and reigns with you and the Holy Spirit, one God, for ever and ever. Amen.   —Proper 8

— QUESTIONS —

Do you know the indwelling presence of the Holy Spirit of God? Or is He an absentee landlord to you?

Can others testify to His presence in your life? Has His glory made a difference?

Are there areas of your life that God is reconstructing right now?

Are there areas that you still need to bring to His attention?

CHAPTER 3

Thirsting for Fulfillment

REDEEMED AND RECONCILED with God—we're on our way! But we are still human, we are still living in this world, so we will still struggle with our faith. It has always been that way. I am always astonished when people who come to faith in Jesus express surprise and dismay that they have to decide over and over again to do things God's way. It's as if they expected to be coated with a shield of some sort that would protect them from their environment and make all their choices easy.

When the world rushes in around us, we can lose sight of those things that give us spiritual strength and sustenance. We may begin to feel that our faith is less and less fulfilling. We thirst for fulfillment, that spiritual fullness that we had at first. We wanted to experience it always, but our needs and our nature slip into the presence of our minds. But we can look in the Scriptures and take heart! The disciples felt exactly this way while Jesus was with them. Let's look at a story from the eighth chapter of Mark:

> Now the disciples had forgotten to take bread, and they did not have more than one loaf with them in the boat. Then He charged them, saying, "Take heed, beware of the leaven of the Pharisees and the leaven of Herod." And they reasoned among themselves, saying, "It is because we have no bread." But Jesus, being aware of it, said to them, "Why do you reason because you have no bread? Do you not yet perceive nor understand? Is your heart still hardened? Having eyes, do you not see? And having ears, do you not hear? And do you not remember? When I broke the five loaves for the five thousand, how many baskets full of fragments did you take up?" They said to

Him, "Twelve." "Also, when I broke the seven for the four thousand, how many large baskets full of fragments did you take up?" And they said, "Seven." So He said to them, "How is it you do not understand?" (vv. 14–21).

Imagine their chagrin. The apostles suddenly remembered that they had left their homes that morning without having packed a lunch. Somewhere in the middle of the day, they were hungry and seemed to have no provision. Jesus took this simple act of forgetfulness as an opportunity to teach them to remember the wondrous works of the Lord.

Their forgetfulness occurred after two incidents that are very familiar to us, Jesus' feeding of large crowds with very little available. Each time, with loaves and fishes, He took what was available, blessed it, broke it, and gave it to fulfill the needs of the multitude. The apostles were witnesses to this. Against the background of their having witnessed God's supernatural provision, Jesus asks His friends, "And do you not remember?"

Remembering is our way to fulfillment. We are like the apostles; we can witness a great act of God, then forget it when another need arises. Most of us have memories that are able to retain many things we ought to forget and forget those things we ought to remember! We see the hand of God provide, and we praise and worship Him at the time. Then a day or two later we find ourselves reacting with fear, complaints, and other behaviors that reflect a faulty memory. We challenge God, "But what have You done for me lately?" We can become dissatisfied with the way God is handling our lives; after all, didn't we give our lives to Him? We have lost some of our confidence in Him.

Remembering God and what He has done for us is the way we rebuild our confidence in Him. Really remembering, continuing to praise Him. Not just recalling what happened, perhaps wondering why things aren't that way now, but recalling, praising, and looking for His hand in our lives again. Remembering with confidence is trust. Trust based on the very nature of God's relationship with us. We have a God who remembers. We have a God who fulfills.

The God Who Remembers

We might summarize the entire Bible as the story of the way in which God has remembered us, in a covenant relationship. God has made the covenant, and it is on the basis of His steadfastness, His trustworthiness, and His faithfulness to His covenant as He remembers it, that we can trust Him with confidence from generation to generation. Our God does indeed remember.

In Genesis 9 we find the account of Noah leaving the ark after the great Flood, which was the judgment of God upon the earth for the wickedness of humanity. God had preserved Noah, his wife, their three sons and their wives in the ark. God gave them instructions as they were beginning their lives on land again, and also gave them a promise:

> Then God spoke to Noah and to his sons with him, saying, "And as for Me, behold, I establish My covenant with you and with your descendants after you, and with every living creature that is with you: the birds, the cattle, and every beast of the earth with you, of all that go out of the ark, every beast of the earth. Thus I establish My covenant with you: Never again shall all flesh be cut off by the waters of the flood; never again shall there be a flood to destroy the earth" (vv. 8–11).

This covenant is wholly God's doing. He established the covenant with Noah, his family, and all the animals. The animals that weren't on the ark perished due to the sin of man (even as they still do today), so God made His promise to Noah and all that Noah had preserved. It was customary in Noah's culture to have some sign of a promise made, something that would serve as a reminder to the parties involved. God set forth His reminder:

> And God said, "This is the sign of the covenant which I make between Me and you, and every living creature that is with you, for perpetual generations: I set My rainbow in the cloud, and it shall be for the sign of the covenant between Me and the earth. It shall be, when I bring a cloud over the earth, that the rainbow shall be seen in the cloud; and I will remember My covenant which is between Me and you and every living creature of all flesh; the waters shall never again become a flood to destroy all flesh" (vv. 12–15).

God gave the rainbow as His sign, a reminder to Him and to His created order that the world would not again be destroyed by water. In making this covenant, He was binding Himself to His creation, limiting His actions, pledging His faithfulness to act in a certain way.

Knowing He would fulfill it, God wanted to be remembered as the God who made a promise.

The Covenant with Abraham

In Genesis 17, we have the beginning of the central story of the Bible: the story where God calls a people to be His own. "And I will make My covenant between Me and you, and will multiply you exceedingly" (v. 2). He further explains: "And I will establish My covenant between Me and you and your descendants after you in their generations, for an everlasting covenant, to be God to you and your descendants after you" (v. 7).

God is making a covenant to take a certain people as His own people. He then sets forth the terms of His covenant of selection: "And you shall be circumcised in the flesh of your foreskins, and it shall be a sign of the covenant between Me and you" (v. 11).

Again, an outward sign is established. God has made the covenant, and there are no strings attached. He has not said, "If you will do this, then I will do that." God has chosen a people for His own, and He pledges Himself to the accomplishing of that purpose.

The covenant made with Abraham was renewed with Abraham's son, Isaac, and Isaac's son, Jacob. Jacob became the father of twelve sons; those sons are called the "children of Israel," because Jacob's name was later changed to Israel. They, in turn, became the fathers of all of the descendants of Abraham. Those descendants eventually went down to Egypt due to a famine, and lived there for four hundred years. During that time they grew into a great multitude and were reduced to slavery. We read of the importance of the covenant to the people of Israel in their captivity:

> Now it happened in the process of time that the king of Egypt died. Then the children of Israel groaned because of their bondage, and they cried out; and their cry came up to God because of the bondage. So God heard their groaning, and God remembered His covenant with Abraham, with Isaac, and with Jacob. And God looked upon the children of Israel, and God acknowledged them (Ex. 2:23–25).

God's covenants are everlasting; the purpose of the covenant doesn't change with the circumstances. When the pain and misery of the bondage of His people caused them to cry out for help, the Lord remembered His covenant. He wanted His people to remember that He had bound Himself to them.

The Covenant with Moses

In Exodus 3 we read that Moses was told by God to go to Egypt, to demand that Pharaoh release the people of Israel. Moses hesitated, and wondered how the people of Israel would respond to his coming to help.

> Then Moses said to God, "Indeed, when I come to the children of Israel and say to them, 'The God of your fathers has sent me to you,' and they say to me, 'What is His name?' what shall I say to them?" And God said to Moses, "I AM WHO I AM." And He said, "Thus you shall say to the children of Israel, 'I AM has sent me to you.'" Moreover God said to Moses, "Thus you shall say to the children of Israel: 'The LORD God of your fathers, the God of Abraham, the God of Isaac, and the God of Jacob, has sent me to you. This is My name forever, and this is My memorial to all generations'" (vv. 13–15).

God said He wants to be remembered as a God who entered into covenant with our forefathers. He wants to be remembered as the God who has offered Himself in covenant to His people. God's faithfulness is the basis for our confidence and fulfillment.

In Leviticus 26 we find the covenant again renewed with Moses. When Moses received the covenant, it involved a great many blessings. Many generations had passed in the four hundred years after Jacob; the people had multiplied, and so had their disobedience. Because of their disobedience, the covenant becomes more specific: "If you obey my covenant [the Ten Commandments] I promise I will. . . ." The blessings of the covenant could, from that time on, be obtained only through obedience.

> But if they confess their iniquity and the iniquity of their fathers, with their unfaithfulness in which they were unfaithful to Me, and that they also have walked contrary to Me, and that I also have walked contrary to them and have brought them into the land of their enemies; if their uncircumcised hearts are humbled, and they accept their guilt—then I will remember My covenant with Jacob, and My covenant with Isaac, and My covenant with Abraham I will remember; I will remember the land" (v. 40).

Did you notice that the names of the patriarchs are mentioned in reverse order? Generally, it's Abraham, Isaac, and Jacob. Here God is reversing the names, reminding the people that He will remember the covenant He made with their forefathers, turning back the trend of the generations. Verse 45: "But for their sake I will remember the covenant of their ancestors, whom I brought out of the land of Egypt in the sight of the nations, that I might be their God: I am the LORD."

God's covenant is always contemporary—remembered by God for the people, who will remember to allow Him to be their God.

The Ongoing Covenant

The purpose of the covenant was so the Lord would have a group of people who knew they were His own in this world. There are millions of people in the world, all created by God, most of whom have no idea of His love for them. God wants a group of people to know His love and to respond to it. He wants them not only to know they have been chosen by Him but to choose Him as well. God has bound Himself to His people in a living, ongoing relationship. He wants His people to remember that, to have confidence in it, and to be fulfilled by it.

In Numbers 15 there is a little vignette in which God calls His people to remembrance. He had given outward signs before in the rite of circumcision and the rainbow; now He devises others:

> And the LORD spoke to Moses, saying, "Speak to the children of Israel: Tell them to make tassels on the corners of their garments throughout their generations, and to put a blue thread in the tassels of the corners. And you shall have the tassel, that you may look upon it and remember all the commandments of the LORD and do them, and that you may not follow the harlotry to which your own heart and your own eyes are inclined, and that you may remember and do all My commandments, and be holy for your God. I am the LORD your God, who brought you out of the land of Egypt, to be your God: I am the LORD your God" (vv. 37–41).

God didn't decide to put tassels on the garments because He liked fancy details, but because He knew that the people needed a reminder. God's purpose is to do anything He can to impress upon His people the knowledge that we are His, that He is our God. The whole point of God's relationship with His people is that mutuality. Those tassels, and later religious adornments, even to today, are to believers much as a wedding ring is to a bride and groom: they are a symbol of their covenant, a reminder that they have chosen one another.

In Deuteronomy 7 we find a beautiful statement of God's feeling toward His chosen people:

> For you are a holy people to the LORD your God: the LORD your God has chosen you to be a people for Himself, a special treasure above all the peoples on the face of the earth. The LORD did not set His love on you nor choose you because you were more in number than any other people, for you were the least of all peoples; but because the LORD loves you, and because He would keep the oath which He swore to your fathers, the LORD has brought you out with a mighty hand, and redeemed you from the house of bondage, from the hand of Pharaoh, king of Egypt. Therefore, know that the LORD your God, He is God, the faithful God who keeps covenant and mercy for a thousand generations with those who love Him and keep His commandments (vv. 6–9).

God has chosen His people out of love, not merit. Sometimes people say that the God of the Old Testament is a God of judgment and the God of the New Testament is a God of love. Such people haven't the faintest glimmer of understanding. God's great love is poured out all through both Testaments; it's what the Bible is about! This great love motivated the covenants, and motivates God's faithfulness in keeping them.

Is it not natural to think that this would be the case on both sides of the covenant? Might it be reasonable to think that those who were loved and chosen by God would, out of love for Him, be motivated to remember and keep the covenant? This is the nature of a mutually fulfilling relationship—trust based on confidence in the love shared. The Deuteronomy passage goes on to recount various blessings in obedience, and then gives a caution:

> If you should say in your heart, "These nations are greater than I; how can I dispossess them?"—you shall not be afraid of them, but you shall remember well what the LORD your God did to Pharaoh and to all Egypt: the great trials which your eyes saw, the signs and the wonders, the mighty hand and the outstretched arm, by which the LORD your God brought you out. . . . You shall not be terrified of them; for the LORD your God, the great and awesome God, is among you" (7:17–21).

Remember

Sometimes we will find ourselves in situations where we are fearful—when it seems as if the opposition is too great for us to deal with—and we may succumb to discouragement or despair. Whenever this happens, Scripture calls us to remember. We are to remember the Lord and what He has done for us, and trust that He will be faithful in all circumstances. Why do we keep waiting for Him to be unfaithful? He is no less able to deliver His people now than He was in the days of old. Why do we expect Him to fail us? He loves us no less than He loved Israel. He promised Himself to us, made a covenant with us, and He will remember His covenant.

We are like the apostles with Jesus on the lake. Jesus needed to ask His fearful disciples, "Why do you reason because you have no bread?" The lack of bread was only a problem in the world's terms. Jesus was really asking, "Why do you assume that the burden of the solution to the situation is upon your shoulders?" That is a question He would ask us today, whatever the circumstances.

Today we can pick up almost any magazine and find articles on how to obtain fulfillment from our jobs, our marriages, our parenting, our hobbies, our homes, our clothing, our investments. If we will follow the writer's advice, we will supposedly come one step closer to the fulfillment we seek. Don't you believe it! The world's solutions, what we do in this world for ourselves, will not bring fulfillment. On the contrary, they will only increase our appetite for more, like salted peanuts increase our thirst but don't fill us.

Jesus asks us some tough questions. "Do you not yet perceive or understand?" Has the understanding of this covenantal relationship become a part of you? Do you put your whole trust in God? "Is your heart still hardened?" Is there still some part of you that resists complete submission to Jesus? Is there some behavior or opinion that keeps you from believing that God's faithfulness and fulfillment will come to you? "Having eyes, do you not see?" Do you give others credit for something God has clearly done? Or circumstances? Or yourself? "And having ears, do you not hear?" Have you never really heard and accepted the declaration of love and faithfulness that God has made to you? "And do you not remember?" Do you tend to disregard those things God has done, and doubt?

In Deuteronomy 15 we find yet another reason to remember: our attitudes are governed by the things we remember. God tells the Hebrew slave owner to remember that he was once a slave in Egypt and to let that memory temper his behavior toward his own slaves: "You shall remember that you were a slave in the land of Egypt, and the LORD your God redeemed you; therefore I command you this thing today" (v. 15).

God didn't suggest we remember; He commanded it. Remember what you were before God intervened in your life! Give testimony to what He has done. If we have been forgiven, we are to forgive. We are to act on what we know of God's interaction with us, to extend the mercy and grace we have received to others. We say this every time we say the Lord's Prayer: "Forgive us our sins as we forgive those who have sinned against us."

The New Covenant

Perhaps the greatest act of remembrance available to us is enacted each time we celebrate the Eucharistic Feast. The words from the celebration are taken directly from Scripture:

> For I received from the Lord that which I also delivered to you: that the Lord Jesus on the same night in which He was betrayed took bread; and when He had given thanks, He broke it and said, "Take, eat; this is My body which is broken for you; do this in remembrance of Me." In the same manner He also took the cup after supper, saying, "This cup is the new covenant in My blood. This do, as often as you drink it, in remembrance of Me" (1 Cor. 11:23–25).

The sign of the new covenant is the holy Communion. It is given to us to help us remember the Lord who gave His life for us. When God's Son died on the cross, His Father took note of it! The death of Jesus on the cross forever removed the penalty for our sin, and God will not forget that. If only our memory of it were more clear! When we approach the table of the Lord, do we think about what this means, or do we think about whether we'll get out of church in time to do something else? The Eucharistic Feast is intended to be a time of rejoicing! We celebrate what Jesus has done for us.

If we have accepted Jesus Christ by faith, and received Him as our Savior, God will never hold us accountable for a single sin we have ever committed. When God forgives, He forgets. He wants us to do the same thing. One of the hardest things for us to do as Christians is to forgive ourselves. So often the sins of the past keep us from fully appreciating the work of God in the present. It's as if we come to the altar of God and give Him all of the garbage of our lives, laying it on the altar so we can feel free for awhile. Then we gradually sneak back and take pieces from the pile, things we somehow feel we can't live without. After all, some of those things have been with us all our lives! If you've ever had a garage sale, you'll know what I mean. The temptation to take the stuff back into the house is tremendous! Well, Jesus has paid the price on the cross for all of the stuff we need to get rid of. We must let Him take it away!

God remembers His covenant but forgets our sins when we partake of the eternal covenant of the cross. Jesus took the loaves and fishes and offered them to God, broke them, and distributed them to meet the needs of the assembled multitude. He wanted the people to remember that God could meet their needs. When He took the bread and broke it, and gave it to his disciples with the cup of wine, He symbolized His broken body and spilled blood, to meet the needs of all who would believe. "And do you not remember?" Do you not remember, when you receive the sacraments, that they are given by a God who loves you, who is faithful to you, who seeks to fulfill you?

There is nothing wrong with God's memory. He didn't need the rainbow in the sky to remind Him of His promise to never again destroy all flesh. He gave the rainbow because He knew it would delight the eyes and hearts of the viewers as they were reminded of His promise, so they could recall Him. God didn't need the sign of circumcision to remind Him of His covenant with the Jews. It was a sign to them of God's special delight in them. God didn't need the tassels on the garments and He doesn't need the crosses or other symbolic Christian ornaments we wear or display today. They are things to remind us of our faith. God doesn't need bread and wine to remind Him that He has promised to forgive all who come to Jesus in faith. They are reminders to us of God's delight in His Son's ultimate sacrifice, of God's delight in us through Jesus, and of God's delight in the glory that will be when Jesus comes again. "For as often as you eat this bread and drink this cup, you proclaim the Lord's death till He comes" (1 Cor. 11:26).

There is a beautiful passage in Isaiah 62 that illustrates the delight of God:

> You shall be called by a new name,
> Which the mouth of the LORD will name.
> You shall also be a crown of glory

In the hand of the LORD,
And a royal diadem
In the hand of your God.
You shall no longer be termed Forsaken,
Nor shall your land any more be termed Desolate;
But you shall be called Hephzibah, [My Delight Is
    in Her], and your land Beulah [Married];
For the LORD delights in you, . . .
And as the bridegroom rejoices over the bride,
So shall your God rejoice over you (vv. 2c–5).

God's covenant of love. Delighting in His people and pledging himself to them. Giving us a new name, as a bride takes the name of her
husband. (At least, some still do!) The image of marriage is as close
as we can come to describing the depth of the devotion and delight that
God has for us. The passage goes on to describe how this marriage
relationship works: "I have set watchmen on your walls, O Jerusalem; they shall never hold their peace day or night. You who
make mention of the LORD, do not keep silent, and give Him no rest
till He establishes and till He makes Jerusalem a praise in the earth"
(vv. 6–7).

God has given His people the assurance of His protection, as a
husband protects his bride. He has set watchmen who will keep reminding Him of His people and their needs, just as a caring friend
would remind a husband of an anniversary or a birthday he might
forget. He has given us permission to continually remind Him, giving
Him no rest until He fulfills all that He has promised.

Do we do it? Not often. Why are we so formal with our God? He
desires all that we are, He wants to be a part of all that we experience.
It is in His fulfilling His promises that we find our fulfillment. When
you were a child and someone promised you something, did you let
him or her forget? Probably not!

A child of my acquaintance discovered a radio-controlled motorcycle that he desired when he was three years old. He asked his uncle to
buy it for him. His uncle consulted the package and saw that it was
recommended for a child age six or older, and explained that to his
nephew saying, "I promise, when you are six I will get it for you."

Well, every time that child saw his uncle over the next three years
the child repeated, "I get my motorcycle when I'm six, right?" On
his sixth birthday, when his uncle walked in the door, the boy an-
nounced, "I get my motorcycle today!" The uncle had the wisdom to

purchase it and hold it for the boy, so that when the time was right, he could have the joy of fulfilling his promise, and his nephew could have the joy of the promise fulfilled. That boy is in college now, and his whole family still delights in remembering that motorcycle.

God delights in fulfilling His promises, and He wants us to keep reminding Him. When the boy reminded his uncle, he was building up confidence! So it is with us. When we remind God of His promises, we build up our own confidence. He knows when it is right to fulfill His promises in our lives. Our difficulty comes from our not knowing when we will receive what He has promised, but isn't anticipation a big part of the joy of receiving? If we have confidence and trust in Him, we know that the promise will be fulfilled when the time is right, and we can live in joyful anticipation from day to day.

Spend some time finding what God has promised you. Anticipate His fulfilling these promises in your life. Remind Him from time to time to build up your confidence. Thank Him when the promise is fulfilled—and remember His faithfulness.

Promises

Do you have doubts and fears? Romans 4:20–21 assures us that we can model Abraham's faith: "He did not waver at the promise of God through unbelief, but was strengthened in faith, giving glory to God, and being fully convinced that what He had promised, He was also able to perform." Be fully convinced!

Are you burdened by a besetting sin? Isaiah 1:18 gives the Lord's invitation: "'Come now, and let us reason together,' says the LORD, 'Though your sins are like scarlet, they shall be as white as snow; though they are red like crimson, they shall be as wool.'" Come to Him, and your sins will be washed away. Come to Him, stay with Him, depend on Him.

Does your life lack direction? God promises in Isaiah 42:16: "I will bring the blind by a way they did not know; I will lead them in paths they have not known. I will make darkness light before them, and crooked places straight. These things I will do for them, and not forsake them." God is faithful to guide us.

Are finances a worry? Jesus assures us in Matthew 7:7–11:

Ask, and it will be given to you; seek, and you will find; knock, and it will be opened to you. For everyone who asks receives, and he who seeks finds, and to him who knocks it will be opened. Or what man is there among you who, if his son asks for bread, will give him a stone? Or if he asks for a fish, will he give him a serpent? If you then, being evil, know how to give good gifts to your children, how much more will your Father who is in heaven give good things to those who ask Him!

Whatever the need, there is no limit to the faithfulness of our God in fulfilling it. There is nothing He has promised that He will not give to those who thirst, then trust. And will you not remember?

PRAYER

Blessed Lord, who caused all holy Scriptures to be written for our learning: Grant us so to hear them, read, mark, learn, and inwardly digest them, that we may embrace and ever hold fast the blessed hope of everlasting life, which you have given us in our Savior Jesus Christ; who lives and reigns with you and the Holy Spirit, one God, for ever and ever. Amen.

—Proper 28

— QUESTIONS —

When was the last time you thought of what God has done for you?

When was the last time you shared God's grace in your life with another?

In what areas of your life do you still expect God to fail?

What are some of the promises from Scripture you would like to remind God He has made?

CHAPTER 4

Thirsting for Peace

IN SEPTEMBER OF 1985, on the weekend that our daughter, Melanie, was to be married, a hurricane came through our area. There was a power shortage in some sections of our town and surrounding towns, which made all the preparations for the wedding a challenge. Visiting friends and family were showering and dressing at the homes of parishioners in nearby towns where there was hot water.

The service was scheduled for 10 A.M., and the electricity did not go on until 9:35, which made our prayer lives a bit stronger! All in all, the wedding went smoothly; the day was sunny and clear.

Watching the media coverage of the storm was fascinating. The advance warning generated much anticipation of the hurricane's arrival. Full-time television and radio coverage was given to tracking the storm; for twelve hours prior to its arrival, we were shown film clips of the devastation left in areas where the storm had passed through on its way to us. When the hurricane actually hit on Friday night, there was noise from the wind and driving rain, many trees were toppled, but there was not the kind of damage that many feared would occur. The anticipation of disaster was worse than the reality of the situation—the fear was worse than the fact. The whole area was dealing with a situation that was not within our power to control. Fear leapt in, which dried up our reservoir of peace. We were thirsting for it, fully expecting something to happen to us. Life often brings uncontrollable situations, which generate a strong thirst for peace.

Jesus and his disciples experienced a similar situation.

Now when He got into a boat, His disciples followed Him. And suddenly a great tempest arose on the sea, so that the boat was covered with the waves. But He was asleep. Then His disciples came to Him and awoke Him, saying, "Lord, save us! We are perishing!" But He said to them, "Why are you fearful, O you of little faith?" Then He arose and rebuked the winds and the sea, and there was a great calm. So the men marveled, saying, "Who can this be, that even the winds and the sea obey Him?" (Matt. 8:23–27).

Jesus asks, "Why are you fearful, O you of little faith?" And the disciples wonder, "Who can this be, that even the winds and seas obey him?"

This incident came at a very important time in the ministry of the Lord. His popularity was on the increase. Everywhere He went, He attracted great crowds, and they followed Him. He was often the center of a great deal of attention. For awhile, this attention was favorable. Some looked upon Him as the Messiah, while others saw Him as a great spokesman for God. Though that reputation raised the suspicion of the religious leaders, the common people usually heard Him gladly. He had to stress the need of "getting away from it all." He told the disciples to get into a boat with Him and cross the sea to the eastern shore of the Sea of Galilee, which was relatively unpopulated.

Jesus had had a busy and exhausting day, and so He fell asleep. What could be more natural than for Him to fall asleep in the gently rocking boat? Then the storm arose. The boat began to be washed over by the waves, but still Jesus slept.

The Sea of Galilee is actually a lake located in the Great Jordan Rift. The Jordan Rift starts at Mount Hermon and extends through the Jordan Valley down into Africa. It is the deepest valley on the face of the earth. The Sea of Galilee is actually six hundred feet below sea level. On the western shore, there are mountains and valleys. The combination of the Jordan Rift, the mountains on the western side, and the table lands on the eastern side (now called the Golan Heights) creates a peculiar kind of wind funnel so that very severe storms can come up quickly and unexpectedly. It's almost as if the winds collect and then all of a sudden burst loose, hitting the water at an angle and stirring it into a raging storm. I've seen it happen; in fact, my wife and I were on a boat during a storm. We could see it coming, but it still hit with a sudden impact that was frightening. The water that had been as calm as glass instantly became a raging sea around us.

As in our experience, the disciples probably had no idea that they were going to be in any peril. I like the way Scripture describes it: "And suddenly a great tempest arose on the sea." Remember, many of the disciples were professional sailors and fishermen. They had lived on that water, and were thoroughly familiar with all of its capriciousness. They knew how to handle a boat, even in the worst of situations, and yet they were frightened. It appeared to them as though the Lord was asleep and that He had no concern for them. "Lord, save us! We are perishing!" they cried.

When Jesus awoke, He did not do anything immediately. He addressed the disciples, saying, "Why are you afraid?" The disciples clearly expected Him to do something—if they hadn't, they would have let Him sleep.

It's an interesting contrast to the story of Jonah. Jonah was also in a boat, seeking to get away from it all. The only difference was that what Jonah was trying to get away from was the will of God. God had told Jonah to go to Nineveh to preach God's word, and Jonah's response had been, "Never! As far as I am concerned, you can wipe the city from the face of the earth. I am not interested in its people repenting. I know them too well—and I know that if they repent, you'll forgive them. And I don't want you to forgive them, so I won't go." And he boarded a boat going in the opposite direction. A great storm arose then, too! The people cried out to Jonah and they said, "What do you mean by sleeping? Cry out to your God! Perhaps your God will give a thought to us, so we won't perish." They wanted Jonah to pray.

The disciples didn't awaken Jesus to pray. They said, "Save us!" as though they clearly expected Him to be able to handle the situation. What could He do? They had seen Him do some pretty wonderful things. That very day, He had healed a leper and healed Peter's mother-in-law, but they had never seen Him handle anything like this.

Scripture says He spoke a word and the sea became calm. Wouldn't you like to know what that word was? The winds ceased, the waters were still, and the disciples looked at one another. Ringing in their ears was the question, "Why are you afraid?" Why, their fear was natural! They were on a boat, and their lives were in danger. Why shouldn't they have been afraid? Yet Jesus seemed to be gently reprimanding them, as though they should have known that nothing would harm them. They had allowed the circumstances to dry up their peace and they called out to Jesus to fill them again.

Many times in our lives it will seem as though Jesus is asleep. It will appear that no one is listening to our prayers, that there is no concern for us from heaven. But Jesus said, "Consider the ravens, for they neither sow nor reap, . . . and God feeds them. Of how much more value are you than the birds" (Luke 12:24). The Lord has not given us fear, but a sound mind and confidence in Him. Jesus is the same yesterday, today, and tomorrow. Even the winds and the waves obey Him. His gentle word still speaks peace. Then why do we worry? Our peace flies because we wage war.

War Fronts

The Bible tells us that people outside Christ are at war. They are at war on three fronts simultaneously. They are at war with God—even converted people fight this war over and over again. Who's in control? Who's sitting on the throne? Romans 5:1 assures us that since we are justified through faith, we have peace with God. That peace is available—Jesus is able to speak peace into our troubled relationship with God. Jesus is the only one who can speak peace to a troubled conscience, because He is the only one who can offer us the forgiveness we need in order to have peace on that front.

The second front on which we wage war is with ourselves. There is stress and turmoil within every heart. There are several people within us all—part of us wants one thing, part of us another, and often the things we desire are in conflict with one another. Commitment to the Lord Jesus Christ begins the healing process of bringing our varied desires into line with the will of God. From a psychological point of view, this is the "unifying of the personality." To use a contemporary phrase, it's "getting it all together." Socrates, 450 years before Christ, made the same point in a prayer that is recorded in one of the dialogues of Plato: "Beloved Pan, or whatever gods there be, grant that I may become inwardly one." This unity is possible only through Jesus Christ, speaking peace on the inward front.

The third front, of course, is war with others. In James 4:1 he asked, "Where do wars and fights come from among you? Do they not come from your desires for pleasure that war in your members?" The Bible tells us that fighting among people and wars among nations are actually the externalization of inward strife. Because man is at war within himself, there is war with others. Have you ever found yourself treating another in a hostile way simply because you are taking your frustrations out on him? There isn't really anything the person has done to deserve your hostility. Have you ever punished your children or your pet more as a release for your own frustrations than because of anything they deserved? Scripture says, only Jesus can speak the peace inwardly that will allow the peace outwardly.

Peace, Protection

We learn a way to obtain the peace Jesus offers from a familiar verse in Philippians: "Be anxious for nothing; but in everything by prayer and supplication, with thanksgiving, let your requests be made known to God" (4:6). Don't hesitate to take your joys and sorrows to the Lord—take every aspect of your life to Him! Take your joys, your sorrows, your successes and failures. Learn to live your whole life in the light of His presence. All the things of which you are proud and the things of which you are ashamed—we are encouraged to bring them all to the Lord "by prayer and supplication, with thanksgiving." And what is the result? "And the peace of God, which surpasses all understanding, will guard your hearts and minds through Christ Jesus" (v. 7).

The miracle of the stilled storm is not an isolated incident that happened a long time ago, rescuing a few fishermen and others from certain death. It is an illustration of the fact that the Lord Jesus Christ has authority in heaven on earth and that even the winds and the waves obey Him. As surely as He spoke peace to that troubled sea, He can speak peace to your heart, inwardly and outwardly.

___ PRAYER ___

Almighty and everlasting God, you govern all things both in heaven and on earth: Mercifully hear the supplications of your people, and in our time grant us your peace; through Jesus Christ our Lord, who lives and reigns with you and the Holy Spirit, one God, for ever and ever. Amen.

—Collect for the Fourth Sunday after the Epiphany

— QUESTIONS —

What storms are brewing or raging in your life?

What word would Jesus need to speak to still them?

Has He spoken it in His word?

Why are you fearful?

CHAPTER 5

Thirsting for Guidance

Oᴜʀ ᴏʙᴛᴀɪɴɪɴɢ ᴘᴇᴀᴄᴇ is often conditional on another thirst being satisfied—the thirst for guidance. Just as the disciples expected Jesus to do something or tell them what to do when the storm came up, people often want to know what to do in the circumstances of their lives. They seek the way to peace; they want reassurance that the guidance they receive is genuine.

When times get tough, most people seek guidance from outside themselves. Some people don't even wait until the times get tough—they seek guidance for nearly every move they make. They spend great amounts of time on the telephone with family and friends seeking advice and counsel. Some folks don't make a move without consulting their psychiatrists. Some don't make a decision without consulting their brokers. Some misguided souls consult their horoscopes or tarot cards. Whatever the methods, these outside sources are little more than the world's security blankets, people or things that will make us feel better about the situation we're in. In some cases, it's just a matter of wanting to have someone to share the blame if things don't turn out right.

Christians aren't immune to this need for guidance. Pastoral counselors, even bad ones, are in great demand. There are many self-help books on the shelves of Christian bookstores that translate successful formulas from the world into Christian language, sometimes bending Scripture to prove a point. All human advice is fallible, because all humans are fallible. No one is right all the time. Unfortunately, people expect their advisors to be right most of the time and are often hurt when they aren't. Of course, in some cases the advice was right but the person doesn't want to follow it, so they will ask someone else who might be more disposed to see things their way. Whatever the circumstances, the thirst is real—it's the ability to satisfy that is elusive.

This thirst for guidance is not an unfamiliar one in Scripture. All throughout the Old and New Testaments are experiences of God's people being led by God. That's a mystical experience to some people. They may read passages in the Bible where it says "The Lord told me" or "The Lord said" and feel that those are exaggerated stories because God has never spoken to them, at least not through their physical ears.

Throughout history, God's people have known that if we believe God has a plan for us and wants us to live according to His will, He will make it possible for us to know what that will is! The thirst for guidance in the heart of the believer is placed there by God himself.

Two Questions

The apostle Paul's testimony of his conversion on the road to Damascus brings to our attention two questions that go hand in hand in terms of our receiving the guidance we seek.

Now it happened, as I journeyed and came near Damascus about noon, suddenly a great light from heaven shone around me. And I fell to the ground and heard a voice saying to me, "Saul, Saul, why are you persecuting Me?" So I answered, "Who are You, Lord?" And He said to me, "I am Jesus of Nazareth, whom you are persecuting." And those who were with me indeed saw the light and were afraid, but they did not hear the voice of Him who spoke to me. So I said, "What shall I do, Lord?" And the Lord said to me, "Arise and go into Damascus, and there you will be told all things which are appointed for you to do" (Acts 22:6–10).

The questions Paul asked are, "Who are You, Lord?" and "What shall I do?" Jesus identified Himself, and assured Saul (shortly to become Paul) that he would be told all things that would be appointed for him to do. The Lord's guidance of Saul was conditional on his obedience to Jesus' direction. If Saul had not gone into Damascus—if in fright he had turned back to Jerusalem—he would not have had the guidance he sought.

Paul had been zealous in carrying out the religion of his ancestors, and he had used his strength and ingenuity to destroy the teaching of

Jesus, casting His followers into prison. He was an enemy of "the followers of the Way," as the Christians were called in those days. He saw the elimination of this pernicious teaching as his personal mission in life. Imagine his surprise at this encounter on the road to Damascus! No wonder he asked, "Who are You, Lord?" The bright light and the voice that no one else could hear must have made him think he was losing his mind.

Once Saul knew it was the voice of Jesus, he had no other choice than to say, "What shall I do?" The second question has no meaning apart from the first. Until people have settled in their minds who Jesus Christ is, and have come to see that He is the Lord of life, designated by God to be supreme in the order of the universe, and that there is some part they have to play in that order, the second question will not truly be answered.

That question won't even arise for people who do not take the claims of Jesus Christ seriously. We cannot acknowledge Jesus as Lord apart from the work of the Holy Spirit within us. It is the function of the Holy Spirit to reveal our need, and to make the identity of Jesus clear. The Spirit of God was working in Paul that day on the Damascus road. In a blinding flash, he saw himself as a self-righteous Pharisee, convinced that he was more righteous than anyone else because of his zeal. In that moment, he knew he was in need of a savior. The Spirit of God revealed to him that Jesus was the One who was able to bring the forgiveness of sins and the gift of new life, and Paul accepted that gift. Along with the gift came the promise of guidance, linked to obedience. It has always been that way, and always will be. God's guidance is possible only through obedience to His revealed will.

The Source of Guidance

Let's look at the experience of another Saul, the first king of Israel. God chose Saul, even though he did not want to be king. He went and hid in the garbage heap, trying to avoid his call. The Spirit of the Lord came upon him, and Saul began his reign in great power and blessing. Little by little, he turned away from the Lord. He no longer followed the Lord's direction, and as a result God rejected him as king. First Chronicles 10:13–14 records the sad end to his story: "So Saul died for his unfaithfulness which he had committed against the LORD, because he did not keep the word of the LORD, and also because he consulted a medium for guidance. But he did not inquire of the LORD, therefore He killed him, and turned the kingdom over to David the son of Jesse."

Saul knew he needed guidance; his trouble came when he turned to the wrong source for that guidance. He consulted a medium, someone who would call up the spirits of the dead. He did not seek the Lord's guidance, and so was judged. The law in Leviticus is very specific about this: "Give no regard to mediums and familiar spirits; do not seek after them, to be defiled by them; I am the LORD your God" (Lev. 19:31).

Again in Deuteronomy, God makes it clear that those who seek His guidance are not to look elsewhere.

> There shall not be found among you anyone who makes his son or his daughter pass through the fire, or one who practices witchcraft, or a soothsayer, or one who interprets omens, or a sorcerer, or one who conjures spells, or a medium, or a spiritist, or one who calls up the dead. For all who do these things are an abomination to the LORD (Deut. 18:10–12*a*).

Isaiah 8:19–20 elaborates on the real issue. "And when they say to you, 'Seek those who are mediums and wizards, who whisper and mutter,' should not a people seek their God? Should they seek the dead on behalf of the living? To the law and to the testimony! If they do not speak according to this word, it is because there is no light in them."

Scripture makes it clear that there are forces at work in the world that are not of God. Spiritualism and other occult practices tap into those forces, calling them forces of darkness. "There is no light in them," Isaiah said. There is a great deal of deceit in these practices—just enough truth to make a person who wants an answer badly enough believe in them. It's not difficult to see why people would want to know the future if they are in a situation that is fearful to them, but the Bible's attitude is clear. God is able and prepared to guide us if we depend on Him.

Much credibility is given to astrology these days. Well-known people have their lives charted, supposedly to guide them. The constellations of stars supposedly divide the heavens into "houses" and one's destiny is supposedly controlled by which house the sun was in and which planets were in the same house when one was born. Yet at best astrology is faulty. It is completely unscientific. The planets that are supposed to influence people's lives do not include Pluto and Neptune, which had not been discovered when the astrological "rules" were formulated. The "constellations" are not natural groupings of stars; they only appear to be when viewed from the earth. Only twelve constellations are mentioned in astrology, but a thirteenth that was in existence at the time astrology began, called Ophiucus, is not mentioned. Scientists now realize that the sun does not spend an equal amount of time in each house—its stays vary between six days in Scorpio and forty-seven in Virgo! Most importantly, over the years the heavens have shifted. So, in spite of the astrologers insisting that someone born in early October is a Libra, anyone looking at the sky could see that the sun was in Scorpio. And people actually base their lives on this stuff!

A lot of media attention was given to the allegation that Nancy Reagan consulted astrologers and advised the President on matters according to their advice. Many Christians were horrified. Their image of the Reagans as a believing couple was shattered. Why? Because Scripture forbids the use of horoscopes. The stars don't have the answers. Isaiah warns:

> You are wearied in the multitude of your counsels;
> Let now the astrologers, the stargazers,
> And the monthly prognosticators
> Stand up and save you
> From what shall come upon you.
> Behold, they shall be as stubble,
> The fire shall burn them;
> They shall not deliver themselves
> From the power of the flame;
> It shall not be a coal to be warmed by,
> Nor a fire to sit before! (47:13-14).

As the Lord had earlier spoken of Jesus through him:

> Thus says the LORD, your Redeemer,
> And He who formed you from the womb:
> I am the LORD, who makes all things,
> Who stretches out the heavens all alone,
> Who spreads abroad the earth by Myself;
> Who frustrates the signs of the babblers,
> And drives diviners mad;
> Who turns wise men backward,
> And makes their knowledge foolishness;

> Who confirms the word of His servant,
> And performs the counsel of His messengers
>   (Isa. 44:24–26*a*).

God wants us to seek our guidance from Him alone. He is capable of guiding our lives. We are not to consult those who are familiar with spirits, or witches; we are not to go to fortune tellers or have tarot cards or tea leaves read. We're not to play with Ouija Boards or read our horoscopes. We are to seek God alone. Guidance from other sources is poison to the spirit. Trying to assuage your thirst for guidance in this way is spiritually damaging and potentially fatal.

Means of Guidance

Often people are still confused once they understand this idea. They are willing to ask God to lead them, but they're not too sure how that guidance is to be received. Several examples are given in Scripture. By no means are these exhaustive; God is endlessly creative!

In the familiar story of Gideon we find him seeking guidance from God in the midst of a siege. Gideon was a judge of Israel, and he was surrounded by the Midianites, the Amalekites, and other enemies who had gathered together to destroy Israel. Gideon asked God if He would lead the armies of Israel against these enemies. He was asking for a sign that God meant what He said.

> So Gideon said to God, "If You will save Israel by my hand as You have said—look, I shall put a fleece of wool on the threshing floor; if there is dew on the fleece only, and it is dry on all the ground, then I shall know that You will save Israel by my hand, as You have said." And it was so. When he rose early the next morning and squeezed the fleece together, he wrung the dew out of the fleece, a bowlful of water. Then Gideon said to God, "Do not be angry with me, but let me speak just once more: Let me test, I pray just once more with the fleece; let it now be dry only on the fleece, but on the ground let there be dew." And God did so that night. It was dry on the fleece only, but there was dew on all the ground (Judg. 6:36–40).

Ever since, constructing some sort of test for God to fulfill as a means of indicating whether or not we should do something has been called "putting out the fleece." It's a very common method, but even though God honored it in Gideon's case, it's not a good way to determine the guidance of the Lord. Why? Because it puts God to the test, and often in Scripture we are told not to do that. We are not to try to bend God to our will in any way. We're not to coerce Him; we're not to try to fit Him into our plan. We're to fit ourselves into His plan! Even Gideon still doubted—he put the fleece out twice, just to make sure that the occurrence wasn't a coincidence.

Another way people have determined the will of the Lord is by casting lots. There are several examples of this in Scripture. Let me say right here that just because it's in Scripture doesn't mean you should follow the example! There are many unfortunate and wicked things recorded in Scripture, and just because they are there doesn't mean they are the will of the Lord.

An example of casting lots is found in the first chapter of Acts. There is a list of eleven disciples, Judas having hung himself. The disciples felt they should select someone to replace Judas so that there might still be twelve, in fulfillment of prophetic psalms.

> And they prayed and said, "You, O Lord, who know the hearts of all, show which of these two You have chosen to take part in this ministry and apostleship from which Judas by transgression fell, that he might go to his own place." And they cast their lots, and the lot fell on Matthias. And he was numbered with the eleven apostles (Acts 1:24–26).

This "chance approach" is still used in many churches. In the Coptic Church, when they elect a bishop or archbishop, they do it by casting lots. They select from all the possible candidates, narrow the list down to six people, and pray. They usually have a small child draw lots, and the one whose name is drawn becomes the new bishop. The assumption is that God lies behind it all. There is much prayer, much seeking of His guidance. They believe He controls the natural universe, and therefore the outcome of the lots.

We used this method in my parish twice, when there were vestry positions to be filled, and we had more good candidates than there were positions. Usually, we have had just the number needed; but on these occasions, we had more. The names were drawn from a chalice after much prayer. One of the women who drew a name later told me that she had the experience of picking up one slip of paper and not being able to draw her hand out of the chalice. She dropped that paper, selected another, and her hand came out easily.

The underlying conviction in the hearts of the people who use this method of determining the will of the Lord is found in Proverbs

16:33: "The lot is cast into the lap, but its every decision is from the LORD." God has honored this method many times throughout the ages, but there is still a better way of determining God's will.

Guidance from the Word of God

God guides His people consistently. Scripture makes it clear that much of the guidance we require is already given to us in the written word of God. If the Bible is God's word, it is the principal source of guidance for decisions that we need to make. That's why it's important for us to know the Scriptures! I am often confronted by people who say that the Scriptures don't have all the answers for life today. "What about nuclear war?" they ask. Well, doesn't Scripture deal with the heart of the matter—the enmity that causes wars? What about the AIDS epidemic? Scripture deals with the fact that the body is to be the temple of the Lord and is therefore holy, not to be abused with drugs and sexual promiscuity. Homelessness? In many places we are told to share what we have with the poor, and to give them shelter. If you want guidance from the Scriptures, you need to get down to the heart of the matter, because that's what God does. He examines the roots to deal with the fruits. The answers are there; the problem is that the willingness to follow is not often found in the reader.

Many argue that the Bible is full of inconsistencies, that it is a human instrument. Those who argue that point are just looking for excuses not to believe, not to follow something that challenges them.

A type of Christian guidance popular today involves the Word of God, but borders on chance. I call it "Bible Roulette"—it involves picking up our Bibles in a panic and saying, "I need an answer, Lord, and I need it now!" Then we let the Bible fall open, close our eyes, and point. Then we take that Scripture as God's answer. Well, sometimes it works and sometimes it doesn't, depending on how much our Bibles are used. Most often they will open to Psalms, Proverbs, or Isaiah, but what if we opened to some of the Old Testament genealogies? Or to the words of judgment in Jeremiah? What if we get something we don't like? Do we try again? Guidance from the Scriptures is not a one shot deal—we need to be consistent in our study of Scripture, be open to the Spirit of God to guide us through it.

The longest psalm in the Bible is Psalm 119. It has 176 verses, and each one mentions the Word of the Lord in terms of guidance. Right from the beginning:

> Blessed are the undefiled in the way,
> Who walk in the *law* of the LORD!
> Blessed are those who keep His *testimonies* . . .
> You have commanded us
> To keep Your *precepts* . . .
> Oh, that my ways were directed
> To keep Your *statutes!*
> Then I would not be ashamed,
> When I look into all Your *commandments.*
> I will praise You with uprightness of heart,
> When I learn Your righteous *judgments*
>   (vv. 1–7, *italics mine*).

Let's look at several individual verses. Verse 11: "Your word have I hidden in my heart, that I might not sin against You." The word of God is an antidote to sin. Verse 24: "Your testimonies also are my delight and my counselors." Where are the counselors we need? In Scripture! And people pay $50 or more per hour for guidance they could have for free. Verse 45: "And I will walk at liberty, for I seek Your precepts." Walking with God is not walking according to bondage to rules and regulations, but freedom—the freedom to be who we are truly meant to be. That's possible only in harmony with the will of God. Verse 54: "Your statutes have been my songs in the house of my pilgrimage." Joy is found in following the will of God.

Verse 93: "I will never forget Your precepts, for by them You have given me life." The word of the Lord gives life to the believer. Verse 103: "How sweet are Your words to my taste, sweeter than honey to my mouth!" Doesn't that remind you of Jesus' words (quoting from the Old Testament), "Man shall not live by bread alone, but by every word that proceeds from the mouth of God"? (See Matt. 4:4.) And familiar to us is Psalm 119:105: "Your word is a lamp to my feet and a light to my path."

Guidance! It is pure and readily available to take care of the thirst for guidance whenever it arises.

Guidance by the Spirit of God

Another way the Lord leads His people is by the direct inspiration of His Holy Spirit. Please understand one thing about the leading of the Holy Spirit—it will never, ever contradict the guidance of the Scriptures.

I have heard people say they believed the Spirit led them to fall in love with someone when they were already married. That is simply impossible, since the Word of God makes it plain that adultery is a sin. The Spirit of God, who is the source of our guidance, would never contradict the written Word of God that He inspired! God speaks with *one* voice. We are never led by the Spirit of God to violate what God has already revealed. That point is often neglected in terms of guidance. We tend to think of guidance as an individual thing. We look upward, expecting revelation to come to us as it did to Saul on the road to Damascus—in a blaze of light. That's not going to happen, at least not as the normative Christian experience, because God has already spoken. He's already given us His statutes and commandments. We are dealing with a God who does not change, or change His mind.

If the Spirit of God has free reign in your life, you don't have to ask whether something is the will of God in every decision you make. He will move in you and incline your heart in such a way as to fulfill His purpose. It's not like putting out a fleece or casting lots.

The faucet that controls the flow of God's guidance to you is within your inner heart. Proverbs 3:5–8 says: "Trust in the LORD with all your heart, and lean not on your own understanding; in all your ways acknowledge Him, and He shall direct your paths. Do not be wise in your own eyes; fear the LORD and depart from evil. It will be health to your flesh, and strength to your bones."

If we trust God in everything, He will lead us in the way He wants us to go. If He is leading, He will remove all obstacles before us, and our path will be smoother. Think of a jungle guide going before us, cutting away the vegetation with a machete, forming a safe passage for us.

The key is trusting Him—having faith. God will never let us be so certain about the events in our lives that we will never need Him! God will guide us, step by step. He doesn't hand us a road map and let us do it on our own. The Spirit of God directs us by inspiring our thoughts with His own—moment by moment—not by audible voices or spelling it out in the stars in the sky.

Guidance Through the People of God

The third way God guides His people is through others. God never intends that we go it alone. He will always lead us to a place where we can grow. Growth often means being stretched and tested by others, being led by others, and leading others.

The writer of Ecclesiastes puts it beautifully.

> Two are better than one,
> Because they have a good reward for their labor.
> For if they fall, one will lift up his companion.
> But woe to him who is alone when he falls,
> For he has no one to help him up.
> Again, if two lie down together, they will keep warm;
> But how can one be warm alone?
> Though one may be overpowered by another, two can
>   withstand him.
> And a threefold cord is not quickly broken (Eccl.
>   4:9–12).

Jesus promised blessings as a result of godly fellowship: "Again, I say to you that if two of you agree on earth concerning anything that they ask, it will be done for them by My Father in heaven. For where two or three are gathered together in My name, I am there in the midst of them" (Matt. 18:20).

We cannot sustain a relationship with God by having it just God and us, no matter how much we may depend on the written Word and the Spirit for guidance. There is no substitute for checking things out with one who has walked in the Spirit longer than we have, who knows Scripture better than we do, whose life we would like to emulate in terms of Christian witness. This is the third part of God's guidance. Think of a three-legged stool: the Word of God, the Spirit of God, and the people of God give balance to your life. Eliminate one of the legs, and you will be off balance.

Trust

With guidance, as in all facets of our life in Christ, any progress we make comes by faith. Faith is trusting God to guide, trusting that His word is true, that His Spirit is present and operative in our lives and in the lives of those He has given us. It is trust that enables us to step out in faith even when the horizon looks bleak.

God's guidance comes when we move, not when we sit still. God has a goal for each venture we undertake, and we need to trust Him to bring it to completion. Think of a sailboat in the water. Trust means we make our sails ready to be filled with the wind of His Spirit. God's guidance is the rudder. His Spirit is the power that enables us to arrive where God wants us to be. The rudder is useless without the wind.

God can't guide a life that is not moving in the power of the Spirit, yet the wind of the Spirit filling our sails without the use of the rudder, the guidance of God, can result in great bursts of power with no direction.

I've known many Spirit-filled Christians who bounce from ministry to ministry. It's as if they have arrived at a destination in their journey through life, looked around, and said, "Is this where you want me, God?" rather than seeking His guidance before they set out. That's not operating in trust—it's expecting God to work blessing out of something begun without Him.

Every time we turn on a faucet in our home to begin the flow of water, we trust that it will come. Trust that the guidance of God will flow into your life through His word, His Spirit, and His people. You will not be disappointed.

PRAYER

O God, the strength of all who put their trust in you: Mercifully accept our prayers; and because in our weakness we can do nothing good without you, give us the help of your grace, that in keeping your commandments we may please you both in will and deed; through Jesus Christ our Lord, who lives and reigns with you and the Holy Spirit, one God, for ever and ever. Amen.

—Collect for the Sixth Sunday after the Epiphany

— QUESTIONS —

In what ways have you sought guidance for your life?

Are you able to find guidance in the Word of God?

What kind of guidance have you received from the Spirit of God recently? Did you check it out with Scripture?

Are there God's people in your life that you can check with to be sure the guidance you receive is balanced?

CHAPTER 6

Thirsting for Security

OUR THIRST FOR GUIDANCE points to yet another thirst—our thirst for security. Life, even at its best, is insecure. The world around us changes minute by minute. At times it seems as if we are like corks bobbing around in a choppy sea. God has provided for this thirst to be assuaged, even as He has provided for the other kinds of thirst.

The apostle Paul has asked eight questions that point to our need and to God's provision for that need:

> What then shall we say to these things? If God is for us, who can be against us? He who did not spare His own Son, but delivered Him up for us all, how shall He not with Him also freely give us all things? Who shall bring a charge against God's elect? It is God who justifies. Who is he who condemns? It is Christ who died, and furthermore is also risen, who is even at the right hand of God, who also makes intercession for us. Who shall separate us from the love of Christ? Shall tribulation, or distress, or persecution, or famine, or nakedness, or peril, or sword? As it is written: "For your sake we are killed all day long; we are accounted as sheep for the slaughter." Yet in all these things we are more than conquerors through Him who loved us (Rom. 8:31–37).

God Works for Good

Paul's first question, "What then shall we say to these things?" refers back to the prior portion of his letter to the Romans. In verse 28 Paul states what could be called a mini-creed for the Christian: "And we know that all things work together for good to those who love God, to those who are the called according to His purpose."

69

Paul is convinced that if the two qualifications in that verse are met, that people love God and are willing to follow His call and purpose, then God will work for good in everything that happens to them. This does not mean that if you love God and follow His guidance, only good things will happen to you. The righteous suffer right along with the unrighteous, and no one knew that better than Paul. The point is, if we love God and walk according to His will and purpose, then in everything that happens, God will work some good. Sometimes we won't see it until many months or years later. But we will see it, and our faith will be strengthened by it. The cross of Christ is the supreme example—man at his worst became the occasion to show forth God at His best.

Paul goes on: "For whom He foreknew, He also predestined to be conformed to the image of His Son, that He might be the firstborn among many brethren" (v. 29). There lies the purpose in all that happens in our lives—that we might be conformed to the image of Christ.

Don't let the word *predestined* throw you. It doesn't mean that God arbitrarily looked over a group of people and selected some to come to Him. It refers to God's infinite nature—His position outside of and apart from what we call time. He knows the beginning and the end. He knows who will come to Him, and, knowing who they are, He predestined the things that would conform them to the image of His Son: "that He might be the firstborn among many brethren."

We are to have a family resemblance to Christ as His brothers and sisters, who share His image and His nature. When people see our faces, they are to see the face of Christ reflected in them. Jesus is the only begotten Son of God; we are adopted into His family. Haven't you known many adopted children who took on the characteristics of the other family members so that you almost forgot they were adopted? This is the way it is to be with our relationship in God's family. Our adoption does not in any way put us at a disadvantage. We are all beloved children; we're all to share in the inheritance from the Father. The J. B. Phillips translation of the Bible makes this point clearly:

> Moreover we know that to those who love God, who are called according to his plan, everything that happens fits into a pattern for good. God in his foreknowledge chose them to bear the family likeness of his Son that he might be the eldest of a family of many brothers. He chose them long ago; when the time came he called them, he

made them righteous in his sight and then lifted them to the splendor of life as his own Son (8:28–30).

It's against that background that Paul asks, "What, then, shall we say to these things?" When you begin to understand what God's purpose is, what He is working out in and through you, you can begin to have the security you seek. God will never desert you. He will bring about His plan for you. He knows exactly what He is doing; you can't slip out of His hand or be snatched out of it. Rather than being like corks bobbing around, we are anchored solidly against any storm of life. What, then, shall we say to these things? All God wants to hear you say is "Thank You." What more can you say to such an act of grace?

God on Our Side

Paul's next question is, "If God is for us, who can be against us?" It's all a matter of degree. If God is on our side, who can stand against us? Well, for one thing, the world in which we live can stand against us. To be at one with the world is to be at enmity with Christ. Many things the world will throw at us will be difficult for us to handle, but those circumstances only become mountainous when we lose sight of the Lord of the mountain.

A good example of God's support is the story of Elisha and the Syrian army. The king of Syria was making war against Israel, and Elisha consistently was able to tell the king of Israel where to go and where not to go to avoid the Syrian troops. Naturally the king of Syria was troubled by this, and he suspected one of his men was a spy. He investigated, and was told that Elisha was the one who was able to tell the king of Israel the places to avoid. The king of Syria sent horses and chariots out after Elisha.

And when the servant of the man of God arose early and went out, there was an army, surrounding the city with horses and chariots. And his servant said to him, "Alas, my master! What shall we do?" So he answered, "Do not fear, for those who are with us are more than those who are with them." And Elisha prayed, and said, "LORD, I pray, open his eyes that he may see." Then the LORD opened the eyes of the young man, and he saw. And behold, the mountain was full of horses and chariots of fire all around Elisha (2 Kings 6:15–17).

When trouble comes, we need to pray that our eyes will be opened to see the chariots of fire all around us. Those who are against us don't have the power to defeat us; their weapons, whatever they may be, are useless. Jesus has said that He will not lose even one whom the Father has given Him. You can't possibly be the exception. Now, *that's* security!

God's Love

Paul's next question contains a remarkable statement of faith. "He who did not spare His own Son, but delivered Him up for us all, how shall He not with Him also freely give us all things?" (Rom. 8:32). How much is God on our side? So much so that He sacrificed His only beloved Son. That kind of love flies in the face of the image of God lurking around waiting to get His hands on us to condemn us. People with such views have not begun to understand the heart of God. We were created out of love and redeemed out of love. God's love was the reason for the foundations of the world; His love gave us freedom of choice. God loved us even while we were sinners.

Jesus' death on the cross is the demonstration, the proof of that love. God has provided not only for our salvation, but for all that we will need to accomplish His will for us. We need to know that is His intention and then receive what He has for us. Too often we think we know what's best for us and we ask for what we want, not for God's will to be accomplished. In God's will is our security.

God's will and God's love come to us without any condemnation. That is what Paul is leading to in his next question, "Who shall bring a charge against God's elect?" He goes on to say, "It is God who justifies."

There is something about love that brings a desire to protect and defend the loved one. Think about some of the experiences of childhood. If someone made a remark about your parents or your siblings, you were ready to fight! Later, during your dating years, if there was someone who was very special to you and anyone made a funny remark or cast that person in a less than flattering light, you were quick to defend. That's the image here. God has loved us so much and at such a cost, He will not allow anyone to bring a charge against us. Any charges that come our way are met by His provision.

As a child, do you remember saying, "Sticks and stones may break my bones, but names will never hurt me!" when someone called you a name? Deep down inside, you knew those names did hurt. They were a form of rejection that you felt at the time. The love of God has absolutely no rejection in it. It is total acceptance. The names He calls you are "beloved," "child," "precious." What names do people call you? Probably nothing to your face, but behind your back, perhaps they call you a "religious fanatic." (A religious fanatic is just someone who loves God more than you do.) Don't worry about being accepted in the eyes of others—you are accepted, loved, and honored by God in His Son.

What about the names you call yourself? Whose goals are you trying to meet? If you bring a charge against yourself, you are challenging God's truthfulness. Perhaps you bear the burden of a sin for which you have not completely forgiven yourself. I frequently encounter this with women who have had abortions—they bear the remorse of their actions within their hearts until they are able to allow Jesus to set them free. The word *remorse* is a very graphic picture; it comes from a French word that refers to carrying a corpse around. It was a form of punishment given to murderers in which the corpse of the person they had murdered was tied to them and they bore it until the decaying body caused them to become ill and die. Jesus bore your remorse on His cross! So who can bring a charge against you? Well, perhaps Jesus? Can He?

Paul's next question asks, "Who is He who condemns? It is Christ who died, and furthermore is also risen, who is even at the right hand of God, who also makes intercession for us" (v. 34). Yes, Jesus could bring a case against you, because He came to earth to die in your place. But what does the passage say He is doing? He is sitting at the right hand of God, interceding for us. He would probably not be doing that if he were condemning us.

Imagine a court of law. There is a judge and a jury, and you are the defendant. The prosecuting attorney brings all kinds of evidence against you. Case after case, all sorts of documented and certified proof of your misdemeanors and major offenses against God are brought forward. There is no question as to your guilt, and your heart begins to sink as you wait to hear the inevitable verdict. When it comes, no one is surprised. The judge, bound by the law, is required to pass sentence.

But imagine instead that the judge gets up from his seat, walks down to you and says, "This one is indeed worthy of death, but I will die instead." Justice will be met—but the judge, not the defendant, dies. That is the picture of what Christ did. He is the judge, but

He is also the Savior. He could condemn, but He won't, because He has already paid the price. In His death He completely drained the wrath of God against the sin of the world. The price has been paid in full, forever. That's a love you can rest in securely.

Who Shall Separate Us?

Well, Paul says, if God is for us, and He wants to provide us with all things that we need, and He's not going to bring charges or condemnation against us, then "Who shall separate us from the love of Christ?" (v. 35). He goes on and gives seven examples: "Shall tribulation, or distress, or persecution, or famine, or nakedness, or peril, or sword?" Might these things lead you to believe you had been abandoned by God?

Perhaps these are difficult situations to imagine in the days in which we live, in the relative comfort we enjoy. Still, these situations exist in our world every day, particularly in the areas we call the "third world." In those parts of the world, thousands of new Christians are born every day. Millions of Christians give testimony to the fact that none of these things can separate us from the love of Christ. These people joyfully sing Paul's next verse: "As it is written: 'For Your sake we are killed all day long; we are accounted as sheep for the slaughter.' Yet in all these things we are more than conquerors through Him who loved us."

Through Him who loved us, we have the security for which we thirst. We are more than conquerors over anything that life can bring our way. If we are living in Christ and for Christ and through Christ, nothing can separate us from Christ. If we are not, then we are already separated from Him. It is just that simple. Who shall separate us from the love of Christ? Only our own wills. Nothing else in heaven or on earth can do it.

Paul summarizes with a great hymn of praise. Can you join in with him? In it you will find all the security you'll ever need. "For I am persuaded that neither death nor life, nor angels nor principalities nor powers, nor things present nor things to come, nor height nor depth, nor any other created thing, shall be able to separate us from the love of God which is in Christ Jesus our Lord" (vv. 38–39).

PRAYER

Almighty and most merciful God, grant that by the indwelling of your Holy Spirit we may be enlightened and strengthened for your service; through Jesus Christ our Lord, who lives and reigns with you, in the unity of the Holy Spirit, one God, now and for ever. Amen.

—Collect of the Holy Spirit

— QUESTIONS —

What is making you feel insecure right now?

Do you feel you love God and are called according to His purpose?

What names do you call yourself? Are they loving or condemning?

Are you separating yourself from the love of Christ for any reason?

CHAPTER 7

Thirsting for Purpose

EVERY YEAR, our parish has a large class of adult con-
firmands. They are given a variety of information about the church
and its place in the world, our particular parish, and their places
within its life. We go through the catechism and challenge them to
address each question, and have a time of questions and answers during each session. The catechism has a portion that says:

Q. Where in the Old Testament is God's will for us shown most
clearly?

A. God's will for us is shown most clearly in the Ten Commandments.

Almost invariably, I am asked questions about the Ten Commandments and their place in our lives. Do we still need to pay attention to
the Ten Commandments? Didn't Jesus say they are summarized in
two—love God and love your neighbor? Aren't they out of step with
life today? How can we understand their application? What is their
purpose, and how does it relate to ours?

The thirst for purpose is evident and persistent.

God has a stated purpose for each one of us as individuals and for
all of humanity as a whole.

In the third chapter of the book of Galatians, the apostle Paul deals
with the purpose of God. He was laying it out clearly for the church
he had founded at Galatia. Understand the context—this was a gentile
church. At the time of this writing, "Galatia" was used in both a
geographical sense and a political sense. Geographically, it referred to

an area in north central Asia Minor, north of Antioch. In the political sense, it referred to a Roman province that included southern districts and the cities of Antioch, Iconium, Lystra, and Derbe.

If the letter was written to the northern area, the church was founded on Paul's second missionary journey and the letter was written on his third journey. If it was written to the south, the church was founded on his first missionary journey and the letter was written after the end of the journey, which would make it the earliest of Paul's letters. In his letter he was explaining many aspects of faith, and trying to counteract teaching that said salvation could be earned. Paul made it clear that by grace alone are we saved. But then the question arose, "What purpose then does the law serve?" (Gal. 3:19). The gentile Galatians were aware that the Jewish believers held to the law of Moses and saw Jesus as the fulfillment of that law. If salvation were by grace alone, why would the law still be applicable?

What do we mean when we speak of God's law? The phrase is used in the New Testament over and over again. The gospel of Jesus is that He fulfilled the law. What did He fulfill? You cannot understand the good news of the gospel until you understand the significance of the law of Moses.

The Law of Moses

The law of Moses is divided into two parts: the moral law, or the Ten Commandments, and the ceremonial law, which had to do with the way sacrifices were offered and life was lived out on a day-to-day basis. The law of Moses was given as a part of the Mosaic covenant, which was an extension of the Abrahamic covenant. God's covenant with Abraham was an agreement that God would give him descendants like the sands of the sea, and that through his descendants would one day come into the world someone who would bring blessing to all the families of the earth. The Abrahamic covenant had no conditions attached. It was renewed with Abraham's son Isaac, and Isaac's son, Jacob; then a long period of time passed until the covenant was renewed again with Moses. With Moses, the covenant became more specific. In the giving of the law, God made it clear that He was giving instruction on how to maintain the blessings and promises of the covenant.

Then the LORD said to Moses, "Write these words, for according to the tenor of these words I have made a covenant with you and with

Israel." So he was there with the LORD forty days and forty nights; he neither ate bread nor drank water. And He wrote on the tablets the words of the covenant, the Ten Commandments (Ex. 34:27–28).

The Ten Commandments were later followed by detailed instructions in Leviticus and Deuteronomy. All of these instructions were part of the law. The law was given and the people were told to obey; it was accompanied by promises of rewards for obedience and threats of judgment for disobedience. For instance, they were told that if they did not keep the law, they would lose the land in which they lived, the land that God had given to them. That happened in 586 B.C., and they didn't get it back until A.D. 1948. They were out of their land for over twenty-five hundred years as a result of their disobedience to the law.

The law was thundered down from Sinai's heights, accompanied by flashes of lightning and claps of thunder. It came in an atmosphere of awe and majesty, for the holy mountain was not to be approached by the people. It was impressive and thorough, but it was a law of externals. In Jeremiah 31 we find a promise that one day God would establish a new covenant.

"Behold, the days are coming, says the LORD, when I will make a new covenant with the house of Israel and with the house of Judah— not according to the covenant that I made with their fathers in the day that I took them by the hand to bring them out of the land of Egypt, My covenant which they broke, though I was a husband to them, says the LORD. But this is the covenant that I will make with the house of Israel after those days, says the LORD: I will put My law in their minds and write it on their hearts; and I will be their God, and they shall be My people" (Jer. 31:31–33).

God makes it clear that His people will still be expected to obey His law, but now the law is to be written on the hearts of His people rather than on tablets of stone.

The New Covenant

When the children of Israel were brought out of Egypt, they were slaves; they had a slave mentality as a group. They were still under a taskmaster—no longer Pharaoh, but now the Lord God—and their relationship was one of servitude, out of necessity. God had to teach His people how to be His people again. The children of Israel had picked up some bad habits in the years they had lived among the Egyptians.

In the relationship of a slave to a master, the assumed response is obedience to commands. Obedience is a learned response, not an automatic one. The Israelites needed to be constantly reminded of their special relationship to God, and of the responsibility inherent in that relationship. In God's providence, as He had promised through Jeremiah, when the time was right, God's purpose was to change the nature of the relationship between Himself and His people. He would change it from Master and slaves to Father and children.

> But when the fullness of the time had come, God sent forth His Son, born of a woman, born under the law, to redeem those who were under the law, that we might receive the adoption as sons. And because you are sons, God has sent forth the Spirit of His Son into your hearts, crying out, "Abba, Father!" Therefore you are no longer a slave but a son, and if a son, then an heir of God through Christ (Gal. 4:4-7).

At the Last Supper, Jesus took a cup of wine and said, "This cup is the new covenant in My blood, which is shed for you" (Luke 22:20). Jesus was introducing the new covenant prophesied by Jeremiah. It was not a new version of a legal relationship with God, attended by threats and promises. Jesus lived and functioned under the law, but He died to bring those under the law into a new relationship with God. How? As adopted children of God.

Through the Spirit of God working within us, our obedience comes from the inside out. One of the things that happens to us when we invite Christ to come into our lives is that the Holy Spirit takes up residence within us from that moment on. The Spirit of God transforms us from slaves to sons. The Spirit of His Son enables us to cry "Abba, Father!" "Abba" is Aramaic for "Daddy." It implies great intimacy and delight in the relationship, rather than the more formal "Father." Any man whose child has welcomed him home with a delighted cry of "Daddy!" will know there is a world of difference between the two terms.

The Purpose of the Law

Well, if we are beloved children of God, do we still need to be told what to do? Even in the human terms, the answer is yes. Parents who do not teach their children right from wrong, who do not enable them to successfully function in the world around them are irresponsible.

God is not an irresponsible parent. The law of God is as applicable under the new covenant as it was under the old.

"For the law was given through Moses, but grace and truth came through Jesus Christ" John wrote (1:17). This statement implies that obedience to the law of God is not just what we do on the outside, but the heart attitude that we have as we obey.

I often tell a story about a little fellow whose actions are typically found in young children in church services. He was about four or five, very active and interested in what was going on under, over, and around the pew. His mother had been trying to distract him, offering him toys, keys, and whispering requests to sit down with little success. Finally his father picked him up and firmly sat him down on the seat, with a glance that said, "Sit!" The little boy looked up at his father and said, "I might be sitting down on the outside, but I'm walking around on the inside!" His sonship was being exercised without the desire for obedience having reached his heart. God wants His people to "sit down on the inside."

God's law tells us what to do. God's grace is available to help us want to do it, and God's truth helps us recognize any heart attitudes that are out of line. God gave us the Ten Commandments so that we could recognize our sinful disposition. If there were no law that kept us from driving through red lights, there would be no problem for us if we did so. The presence of the law makes the disobedience of the law a transgression against it. The presence of the Spirit of God within us makes it possible for us to keep the law of God, and to know when we have transgressed.

God knew when He gave the law that we would not be able to keep it ourselves. There is a basic defect in our human personality that, when we are told to do something, makes us resist, and when we are told not to do something, makes that thing automatically irresistible. The law, rather than encouraging obedience, actually challenges the rebellion that is in our hearts. God knew this, and gave the law to increase the rebellion. "Moreover, the law entered that the offense might abound. But where sin abounded, grace abounded much more, so that as sin reigned in death, even so grace might reign through righteousness to eternal life through Jesus Christ our Lord" (Rom. 5:20–21).

The Law in Our Hearts

We are told that the law is a perfect expression of the will of God. Our God is a changeless God. The will of God for His people today is the same as it was in Moses' day. When Christ came, we received the Spirit of God to work out obedience to the law because we wanted to be obedient, not because we feared retribution of some sort. Paul explained, "Therefore, my brethren, you also have become dead to the law through the body of Christ, . . . we have been delivered from the law, having died to what we were held by, so that we should serve in the newness of the Spirit and not in the oldness of the letter" (Rom. 7:4a, 6). If we are serving in the newness of the Spirit, we will of course fulfill what the law of God requires, since the Holy Spirit would not contradict the will of God. The law of God does not change. The only difference is that instead of being an external force in our lives the law is an internal force—a yielding of our hearts, minds, and wills to the will of God.

Isn't this the way we raise our children? At a certain point we must exercise absolute and external authority over them, when they are not able to reason and choose. As they mature, we let what they have learned gradually become the basis for their making informed, independent choices. Sometimes they'll make the wrong choices, and suffer the consequences, but there is always forgiveness and love awaiting them. Our purpose is to help them grow and become responsible citizens of the world and the kingdom of God. That is exactly the model that God uses with us.

The Law of God

Jesus summed up the law of God as falling into two distinctions— loving God and loving your neighbor as yourself. Let's look at the Ten Commandments in these terms, and think about how the new covenant's grace and truth might see them lived out in today's world.

Loving God

1. *You shall have no other gods before Me.* The late Paul Tillich was a famous theologian and I was privileged to have studied under him. He used to say that God was "man's ultimate concern." This meant that whatever is the prime focus of your life, your ultimate concern, is your god—whatever that is! If it isn't the God of Abraham, Isaac, and Jacob, the Father of our Lord and Savior Jesus Christ, then you are having difficulty with this first commandment. God will not share His worship with another—either in addition to Him or in opposition to Him. You must choose. The indwelling Spirit of God will enable you to change your priorities to make God first on your

list. Once this happens, and God is your ultimate concern, you will find that the other nine commandments are much easier to keep.

2. *You shall not make for yourself a carved image—any likeness of anything. . . . you shall not bow down to them nor serve them.* God knows humanity's need for security. Somehow it is easier to remember to be obedient to a God who seems tangible, touchable—one you can hold onto. Yesterday's idols were cast in bronze and wood. Today's carved images and likenesses are most often found on green slips of paper folded up in our pocket, small pieces of plastic that we exchange for goods, or multi-colored stock certificates. The more of these that we have around, the more secure we seem to feel. Yet the Spirit of God can enable us to keep those pieces of paper and plastic in the right perspective—as things to be used to bring God glory. We are not to bow down to them. We're to make life's decisions based not on the fiscal bottom line, but on God's direction. We're not to serve these idols by spending more time seeking them than we do with our families or with God. We're to desire them as means, but not as ends for our lives.

3. *You shall not take the name of the* LORD *your God in vain.* We hear the name of Jesus used in conversation on the street every day. I wonder why that precious name has become the primary expression of anger and frustration, of pain and desperation in today's culture? That is an abomination to the Lord, and the Spirit of God is the only thing that will enable you to break that habit or to encourage others to do so. When that name is precious to you, you will defend and protect it, and use it in praise and thanksgiving.

Did you ever wonder why in an oath of office those taking the oath are asked to raise their right hand toward heaven, then to say the oath ending with, "So help me, God"? This practice recognizes that the name of God is holy, and that any promise, intention, or oath can be accomplished only by His aid.

4. *Remember the Sabbath day, to keep it holy.* This is both a practical matter and a spiritual one. God knows the composition of his people—their tendency to overdo and to neglect themselves and their relationship with Him. By declaring a sabbath day, a day when the cares of the world are set aside and He is the focus, God is enabling us to come together and be refreshed in Him, to be prepared for the work

He has for us to do in the days ahead. The time is holy, set apart for His use. Let Him be reflected in that day's activities! Seek His face, and then seek His will for using the time of that one day out of seven.

Loving Your Neighbor

5. *Honor your father and your mother, that your days may be long upon the land which the* LORD *your God is giving you.* "Honor" has many faces, most of them seldom seen in today's society, yet most sociologists realize that proper family structure gives structure to society as well. Honor can be used in terms of loyalty, for instance. People often blame their parents for the problems they have coping with life. Somehow that's easier than accepting responsibility and dealing with the problems themselves.

"Honor" in terms of respect is difficult to recognize. Our parents are to have a place of distinction in our lives. We are to show regard for them, to accept them with all their faults, and to grow in grace through or in spite of our relationships with them. That is only possible through the indwelling of the Holy Spirit. The Holy Spirit helps us realize that God chose those parents for us. We had no say in the matter, nor did they have a say in who we would be! It's strange how we expect unconditional love from our parents as we grow up, and don't remember to exercise that same degree of love toward them when we are no longer dependent upon them. Our heart attitude is of utmost importance here. A child who puts his parent in a care center and doesn't visit is fulfilling the letter and not the spirit of the law.

This commandment is the only one that carries a promise. Chances are, if our days are long in the land, we will be parents whose children will model their relationship with us on the relationship they saw us exercise with our parents.

6. *You shall not murder.* The old covenant made a clear distinction between accidental death and deliberate action. Jesus went even further in explaining this commandment, saying that if you hated, you were disobeying the law, because hate is a deliberate decision that you make against someone. Racial, economic, religious, or sexual prejudice all would be classed under this commandment.

Abortion is murder. So is euthanasia. God did not say you could have an exception from this law if it was inconvenient to begin or to continue a life. War, capital punishment, and the deliberate political actions that make for starvation and deprivation in many societies in

the world today are all results of the disobedience of this commandment. Knowing the Lord Jesus Christ is the only means of righting the
myriad of wrongs that stem from disobedience to this commandment.

7. *You shall not commit adultery*. Or lust in your heart, either!
Faithfulness within and chastity outside of God's established covenant
of marriage is His acceptable standard. His reason for this standard is
linked to the nature of His relationship to us, for in many places in
Scripture God uses the image of marriage to describe His love for His
people. But God is also practical. God knows the human heart, and
He knows how difficult it is to achieve true intimacy in a relationship.
It takes commitment and time, and is well worth the effort. It is not
found in casual encounters that satisfy immediate urges but not our
deepest needs. It is the Spirit of God within us that enables the desires
of the flesh to be properly channeled both outside and inside marriage. Remember that God sees the heart attitudes here as well. Is it
being faithful to your spouse to tear him or her down in front of others
or behind his or her back? The Spirit of God will change your
thoughts as well as your actions.

8. *You shall not steal*. This commandment doesn't just refer to
stealing goods from another. It also refers to taking credit for work
done by another, cheating on your income taxes, and not paying your
bills if you are able to do so. It refers to the nature of the relationships
we have with one another, keeping things honest and aboveboard. It
refers to paying wages properly to an employee, and to an employee's
need to not defraud an employer of the work or goods he or she is
paying for by using office time and equipment for personal pursuits.

9. *You shall not bear false witness against your neighbor*. This
isn't just in terms of testifying in a court of law. It refers to testifying
in the court of the neighborhood, or the office, or the church. Wher-
ever you would speak of another, make sure that your witness is true
and clear of any slant toward your own interests as opposed to another's. The heart attitude God desires here is humility.

10. *You shall not covet . . . anything that is your neighbor's*. Many
people have told me that they can, by the grace of God, make it
through the first nine commandments. But when it comes to the tenth,
they are in trouble. Few people are satisfied with their lives just as
they are. They constantly see others who have something that they

want. This commandment deals directly with the desires of the heart. It deals with our being able to live as God intends us to live, in an attitude of thanksgiving for who we are and what He has given us.

God's purpose in His law, then, is to help us recognize those things in us that we need to bring before Him, asking His help to be more like Jesus. I'm not setting yet another set of rules in front of you, saying, "If you're going to be a good Christian, you've got to pray." No! If you are yielded to the Holy Spirit, you will pray because you want to pray. I'm the last one to tell you that if you want to follow Jesus, you've got to go to church at least once on Sunday. If you yield to the Holy Spirit, He will lead you into fellowship with God's people and you will desire corporate worship. I'm not saying you have to tithe, but if you yield to the Spirit, He will help you to understand that all your possessions belong to God, and you might start asking yourself what you are entitled to keep! That's altogether different. Don't let people tell you that you've got to witness if you're a Christian. Yielding to the Spirit will give you a desire to tell others what God has done in your life, and it will be natural and winsome to those whom you speak.

Do you see? The answer of Christianity is "no" to rules and regulations that are imposed from the outside, and a "yes" to the Spirit who flows through us from the inside out, leading us to drink from the well of living water, quenching our thirst for purpose.

PRAYER

O God, you made us in your image and redeemed us through Jesus your Son: Look with compassion on the whole human family; take away the arrogance and hatred which infect our hearts; break down the walls that separate us; unite us in bonds of love; and work through our struggle and confusion to accomplish your purposes on earth; that, in your good time, all nations and races may serve you in harmony around your heavenly throne; through Jesus Christ our Lord.
Amen.   —Prayer for the Human Family

— QUESTIONS —

What is your ultimate concern?

Which of the Ten Commandments do you usually have the most difficulty keeping?

What would it mean for you to keep a sabbath day?

Are there heart attitudes that you need to bring in line with God's purpose?

CHAPTER 8

Thirsting for Equality

IN 1776, A GROUP of men gathered together in Philadelphia to produce what is one of the most remarkable documents ever written in the history of the world. The second paragraph began, "We hold these truths to be self-evident, that all men are created equal, that they are endowed by their Creator with certain unalienable rights, that among these are life, liberty, and the pursuit of happiness."

The belief that forms the foundation of what has become the strongest nation in the world arose from a desire to quench a very basic human thirst for equality.

The assurance of equal opportunity and equal protection under law has been a mainstay of the government of the United States for over 200 years—yet we still haven't got it quite right. As people have pointed out in the centuries since, it is not all that self-evident that all are created equal. Some have more talent than others, some have more motivation, some are better looking, some are more intelligent, and so forth. However, those who deny the equality of human beings are missing an important point that the writers of the Declaration of Independence did not miss: the existence and endowment of a Creator.

What does it really mean to be "created equal"? To answer this question, we must look at a series of questions that are asked by the apostle Paul in his letter to the church at Corinth. "For who makes you differ from another? And what do you have that you did not receive? Now if you did indeed receive it, why do you boast as if you had not received it?" (1 Cor. 4:7).

There are two places where all people ought to be equal. One is before the law of the land. Whether we are rich or poor, the bar of justice is to be a level place. Our laws were designed that way. Because they are administered by fallible human beings, it often does not work out that way. Many have found the American justice system to be too lenient, allowing criminals to return to society too quickly, or too harsh, imprisoning an innocent person for a length of time without having carefully established his or her guilt.

The second place where we are all equal is at the foot of the cross. All who stand there stand as guilty sinners. It does not matter whether we are attractive sinners, educated sinners, cultured sinners, or straight from the gutter sinners, we are all on equal footing with God. That is the only certainty we have of equality in life.

One of the peculiarities of our human nature is that we often take pride in things over which we have no control. Physical attractiveness, for instance, or other circumstances of birth such as inherited wealth, fine intellect, an artistic talent of some sort—we determined none of those things. The circumstances of our lives—events and opportunities, fortuitous or difficult—all come to us as gifts. We did not choose to be born in the United States, yet that fact alone has given most of us advantages we would not have had if we had been born in another country. We did not choose to be born in this particular time in history, nor did we choose the parents we have. All these things are gifts from God. So, Paul asks, "Who makes you differ from one another?" The answer is, "God." He has made us as we are to accomplish His purpose in and through us. He sees our potential and our failings. He puts us together with others so that our strengths and weaknesses can be balanced by the strengths and weaknesses of others in order to extend His reign on the earth.

The Bible is very clear about our human nature. In a number of places, it points out three things about which people are most often proud. Jeremiah records the words of the Lord: "Let not the wise man glory in his wisdom, let not the mighty man glory in his might, nor let the rich man glory in his riches" (9:23).

"Glory" is used both as a noun and a verb, and here it is used as a verb. It implies boasting or pride. God, who knows the hearts of His people, realizes that there are three sources of boasting that separate His people from Him and from each other. There are three things which, in the eyes of the world, seem to set some of us above others.

Wisdom

The first is wisdom. "Let not the wise man glory in his wisdom." This response seems almost inevitable. There is something about receiving a fine education that tends to give the person who has it a sense of superiority, a tendency to look down on people who are not as well-versed.

A cartoon in our parish office depicts a sign on the door with someone's name on it, followed by a string of degree abbreviations— M.Div., D.Min., PH.D., D.Lit., and then the line: "your humble servant." Its humor lies in recognizing the fact that there is no degree for humility, and that many degrees tend, as Paul said, to "puff up" our worth in the eyes of ourselves and others.

I'm not trying to minimize the significance of an education. I'm merely pointing out the danger of allowing education to pull us further from God's purpose. "The fear of the LORD is the beginning of wisdom, and the knowledge of the Holy One is understanding," the writer of Proverbs reminds us (see 9:10). If you have received a fine education, thank God for it, and use it to His glory, to benefit others. Do not use it for your glory to merely benefit your sense of self-importance. Education is not wisdom unless it benefits others.

The wisdom of Solomon was given to him by God. He asked for this gift in sincere humility, so that he could lead God's people. He didn't say, "I'm the son of the king, have received the best education possible, and know what's best," and proceed to make rules and regulations. He said, "I am like a little child who doesn't know how to go out or come in out of the rain! I need your wisdom, God." And it is recorded: "And God gave Solomon exceedingly great understanding, and largeness of heart like the sand on the seashore" (1 Kings 4:29). A large heart implies loving generosity—a caring for others. So often people with fine educations lose touch with the people their wisdom is to benefit!

But even great wisdom is not enough to satisfy the thirst in our hearts. Solomon found this to be true. He wrote in Ecclesiastes:

> I communed with my heart, saying, "Look, I have attained greatness, and have gained more wisdom than all who were before me in Jerusalem. My heart has understood great wisdom and knowledge." And I set my heart to know wisdom and to know madness and folly. I perceived that this also is grasping for the wind. For in much wis-

dom is much grief, and he who increases knowledge increases sorrow (Eccl. 1:16–18).

Sometimes things occur in life for which there are no answers, things that are beyond our human capacity to understand. That is where faith comes into the picture. Without a living relationship with the living God, a well-educated person is only more aware of the unanswerable questions, of the futility of the debating process. "Where is the wise? Where is the scribe? Where is the disputer of this age? Has not God made foolish the wisdom of this world?" Paul asks (1 Cor. 1:20).

God stands in opposition to those who take pride in the knowledge they possess, if that knowledge is a thing that separates them from others. God resists the proud and gives grace to the humble. In the wisdom of God, people do not come to a knowledge of Him through wisdom. If they did, only the smart people could come to Him. But Paul goes on to explain, "For since, in the wisdom of God, the world through wisdom did not know God, it pleased God through the foolishness of the message preached to save those who believe" (v. 21).

Believing, through the foolishness of the message preached, is the way God has chosen to save His people. Had I been God, I would not have done it that way. I would never have allowed the salvation of anyone to hang on the slender thread of human preaching. That is as fallible a tool as there ever has been! But God knows what it takes to arouse a response in the hearts of His people. And when they respond in faith, they find life.

It's not through wisdom that people come to the knowledge of God and their absolute equality before Him. It's not through endless arguments of fine points of theology that they will find a humble heart. The doorway into the kingdom is so low down that one must bend in humility to get through. I've never known a single person who has been convinced of the kingdom of God through head knowledge—a person just can't think his or her way into the kingdom of God. Nor can anyone come into the kingdom of God based on a religious experience. It is knowledge of and faith in Christ that enables the equality of life in the kingdom to be real. "For Jews request a sign, and Greeks seek after wisdom; but we preach Christ crucified, to the Jews a stumbling block and to the Greeks foolishness, but to those who are called, both Jews and Greeks, Christ the power of God and the wisdom of God" (vv. 22–25).

Paul goes on to reflect that many ordinary, uneducated people accept Christ and most intellectuals do not; in fact, they argue against the reality of the faith.

> For you see your calling, brethren, that not many wise according to the flesh, not many mighty, not many noble, are called. But God has chosen the foolish things of the world to put to shame the wise, and God has chosen the weak things of the world to put to shame the things which are mighty; and the base things of the world and the things which are despised, God has chosen, and the things which are not, to bring to nothing the things that are; that no flesh should glory in His presence (vv. 26–29).

The Lord overturns human expectation. Over the years I have heard the testimony of educated persons who could not come to faith until circumstances in their lives made them realize they had no power in themselves. I've also heard the testimonies of people who were the castoffs of society—who by the power of God have been given new lives in Christ. God made us differ from one another, but overeducated or underprivileged, God provided just one answer for us all—Jesus. We are all sinners in need of a savior, all equal at the foot of the cross.

Authority

The second basis for human pride that was named by Jeremiah is might. "Let not the mighty man glory in his might." This is the pride of one's position, what one has attained in this life. The mighty are those who stand in positions of authority, who govern from the top down, whose decisions influence the destiny of untold numbers of people and whose dealings trade in untold millions of dollars, at least on paper.

There is an innate desire in many hearts to dominate, to control, to be in a position to rule and govern. It's called the "pecking order"—there are different levels of authority in the world, each pecking down on the level beneath.

Now, there is nothing wrong with having authority. In fact, the Bible makes it very clear that if you have achieved a level of authority, you have done so by the grace of God. God has exalted you, and it is something for which to be grateful, not prideful. But with that authority comes a responsibility. There is something about the human heart that is susceptible to temptation when authority is thrust upon us.

People somehow begin to feel that they are above the law, that they are able to do what they want. They have a delusion that they can act as they please, without regard for others. That becomes very dangerous, especially when the decisions that are made will directly impact the lives of others.

The Bible has a lot to say about those who have authority. Matthew 20:20–28 contains a record of a very human incident, one all mothers can understand. It involves the mother of the sons of Zebedee, James and John. She wanted Jesus to command that one of her sons could sit at the right hand of Jesus and the other at the left. She wanted her sons to have positions of authority and respect in the kingdom of God. Well, you can hardly blame her, but you can also imagine how the other apostles felt when they heard about this! The gospel says they were indignant with the two brothers. The two brothers themselves were probably mortified, and had to make many excuses for their mother. But Jesus' answer to their mother was interesting:

> You know that the rulers of the Gentiles lord it over them, and those who are great exercise authority over them. Yet it shall not be so among you; but whoever desires to become great among you, let him be your servant. And whoever desires to be first among you, let him be your slave—just as the Son of Man did not come to be served, but to serve, and to give His life a ransom for many (John 20:25–28).

That is the basis for equality in the kingdom of God. We strive not to be above one another, but to serve one another. The terms *servant* and *slave* are not part of the vocabulary of this century. The terms represent one with absolutely no rights at all, not even those the Declaration of Independence declared unalienable—Life, Liberty, and the Pursuit of Happiness. Jesus gave His life, and in doing so He gave us liberty to choose to be His servants. If we pursue Him, we will know joy and fulfillment, but not necessarily happiness. Happiness is getting what you want, while joy is wanting what you get. Sometimes what you get is not what you expected. Many persons can tell of being on the top of the corporate heap one day and out pounding the streets the next. Earthly authority is fleeting at best. Without a living relationship with the source of all authority, and a recognition that the authority we exercise is a gift, our sense of self-esteem can dry up the instant our circumstances change. Those who speak and act in the authority of Christ will find a meaning for life that transcends all circumstances. Jesus' life and death was the example. His glory came in opposition to the glory of the might of this world: Jesus, the one to whom all authority has been given, in heaven and on earth.

Riches

Jeremiah had a third basis for the pride of humanity—riches. God warned, "Let not the rich man glory in his riches." I suppose I really don't have to tell you about this kind of boasting—we see it on television every day. It's what sells lottery and sweepstakes tickets; it's what makes media heroes out of people. All this attention ignores the fact that God has prospered that person, has given him the power to obtain the wealth that he has. Deuteronomy makes it very clear:

> Beware that you do not forget the LORD your God by not keeping His commandments, His judgments, and His statutes . . . lest—when you have eaten and are full, and have built beautiful houses and dwell in them, and when your herds and your flocks multiply, and your silver and your gold are multiplied, and all that you have is multiplied; . . . then you say in your heart, "My power and the might of my hand have gained me this wealth." And you shall remember the LORD your God, for it is He who gives you power to get wealth (Deut. 8:11–12, 17–18a).

Having wealth is not condemned. What is condemned is the attitude that having it makes us different from others, better than others. The apostle James speaks of this in the second chapter of his letter:

> My brethren, do not hold the faith of our Lord Jesus Christ, the Lord of glory, with partiality. For if there should come into your assembly a man with gold rings, in fine apparel, and there should also come in a poor man in filthy clothes, and you pay attention to the one wearing the fine clothes and say to him, "You sit here in a good place," and say to the poor man, "You stand there," or "Sit here at my footstool," have you not shown partiality among yourselves, and become judges with evil thoughts? Listen, my beloved brethren: Has God not chosen the poor of this world to be rich in faith and heirs of the kingdom which He promised to those who love Him?" (James 2:1–5).

One of the most effective churches I know of exists in the heart of New York City. Homeless abound in that area, and many of the churches have shelters that feed, clothe, educate, and house the homeless. Most of these good works are done during the week, and so the congregations who worship there have little contact with the homeless except when they sign up to work for a few hours helping out with the program.

Not in this church. In this church they welcome the homeless into their midst. Those with mink coats worship alongside those with mismatched shoes. There are toothless, unkempt seekers in the adult and youth confirmation classes; children who seldom see three meals a day are in the Sunday school and in the Scout packs. People who have slept in the streets because the shelters were full sing in the choir and hands that have clutched newspaper blankets distribute hymnals and service leaflets. People wearing rich perfume kneel for communion at the altar beside those who smell of cheap wine. In that congregation there is a real recognition that it is the grace of God that enables any of us to kneel before God.

James reminds us that making distinctions among ourselves is not God's desire for us. Often, however, even in the church, people who are wealthy are sought out to be put on committees or to serve as trustees in name only. The people who do this seek to benefit from an association with someone of influence, not realizing that the person of wealth may be as spiritually needy as a person who has nothing. A clergy associate of mine calls these people "up-and-outers." They need the gospel of Jesus as much as the downtrodden. That is what enables the rich to worship next to the poor—their common need for the gospel has brought about a sense of equality that no act of charity or social conscience could bring about.

Jesus refers to this need in his dealing with the rich young man who asked what he could do to inherit eternal life. Jesus ascertained that the young man was already observing the law of Moses, and said, "One thing you lack: Go your way, sell whatever you have and give to the poor, and you will have treasure in heaven; and come, take up the cross, and follow Me" (Mark 10:21). The young man was sadly grieved, for he had great possessions. Then Jesus looked around and said to his disciples, "How hard it is for those who trust in riches to enter the kingdom of God!" (v. 24).

Jesus said this because He knew that it is hard to trust in God when we appear to have everything we need. But how secure are securities? Ask anyone who has lost in the stock market. "Riches are not forever," Proverbs warns. If we have our sense of self invested in our investments, we stand to lose all when a crash comes.

From God, for God

If we have been given much in terms of education, authority, or riches, God expects us to use them to benefit others. "For everyone to whom much is given, from him much will be required; and to whom much has been committed, of him they will ask the more" (Luke 12:48).

For rich or poor, God's law is a law of equality. It is a sword that cuts through our pride and prominence to the heart of the matter— "all have sinned and fallen short of the glory of God." Yet there is something in which we can glory, something in which we can take pride and something of which we can boast. God has spoken through the prophet Jeremiah: "'But let him who glories glory in this, that he understands and knows Me, that I am the LORD, exercising loving-kindness, judgment, and righteousness in the earth. For in these I delight,' says the Lord" (9:24).

Our glory is in knowing and understanding the Lord, that He is loving and kind to us all without partiality, and that His judgment is righteous to all of us equally. Our lives and everything in them are gifts from God. We can't depend on the circumstances of life to remain constant, but God is the same yesterday, today, and forever. The wisdom, authority, and riches in the world's terms are mere mirages, not pools of refreshment in life's desert times. Only knowing and understanding God will give us the sense of the equality by which we were created. It can't be legislated or taught, earned or bought. It is a gift of grace from the God who gives us all things.

PRAYER

O God, who created all peoples in your image, we thank you for the wonderful diversity of races and cultures in this world. Enrich our lives by ever-widening circles of fellowship, and show us your presence in those who differ most from us, until our knowledge of your love is made perfect in our love for all your children; through Jesus Christ our Lord. Amen.
—Thanksgiving for the Diversity of Races and Cultures

— QUESTIONS —

What things do you take pride in?

Wisdom, understanding, or largeness of heart—which do you value more?

Are you satisfied with the riches God has given you?

Would authority or servanthood identify your attitude towards others?

CHAPTER 9

Thirsting for Unity

A FEW YEARS AGO, a wonderful charitable move was made by people in the musical entertainment industry to aid the thousands starving in Africa. Many singers and musicians got together and cut a record, the proceeds of which raised many millions of dollars for food. The song was "We Are the World."

I will never forget the first time I saw the size and variety of the group. Talk about unity in diversity! Folk singers, rock singers, gospel singers, country and western singers, instrumentalists of all sorts —all ages, all ethnic heritages—came together to make music. Since that USA for Africa release, other cooperative concerts have been held for various needs in the world—hunger, homelessness, AIDS. What makes these efforts work so well? They communicate the sense that no matter what the problem is, we are all involved in it together and every one of us is needed to achieve the solution. They tap into our innate thirst for unity. "Behold, how good and how pleasant it is for brethren to dwell together in unity!" the Psalmist wrote (Ps. 133:1). And how rare, I might add.

Humanity suffers from disunity. Countries with common borders wrangle with one another over resources. Cities strive against one another for available funding. Companies compete for market share. The churches of Christianity have split and splintered into many factions and sub-factions. Families break up and reorganize. In all the skirmishes, disunity leaves behind numbers of participants who have been wounded in some way. As they recover from their wounds, there is a tendency toward self-protection and self-defense. When those involved are questioned about the situation, the answers are seldom positive and often harshly negative. Out of a painful realization that a relationship that once existed is no longer viable come words of judgment. It is quite a human tendency—one of our great failings, really. We're quick to form evaluations and to come to conclusions, often on the most subjective evidence. This tendency is recognized by the apostle James, who asks, "Who are you to judge another?" (James 4:12*b*).

Faulty Judgment

When I say it is a cloudy day, that statement is a judgment I have made based on evidence. It carries with it no sense of approval or disapproval, unless you hear a particular voice inflection. It's merely a statement, a judgment that has been made on the basis of very gray skies. Now, it's one thing to make a flat statement, but rarely does that happen. Usually there is some indication of approval or disapproval. If I wanted it to be sunny for a particular reason, I might state that it's a cloudy day with a sense of disappointment being expressed. On the other hand, if I wanted it to rain, I might state that it was a cloudy day with a bit of excited anticipation. You would have to know how to read my voice inflections and perhaps my facial expression to know what I was really communicating. Even then you would often be wrong, because sometimes my outward expression does not express my true self—no doubt it is the same for you. That's one of the problems with making a judgmental statement. The way it is said is not necessarily the way it is understood.

Another reason we are told not to judge one another is because we never have all the facts. No matter how well we may think we know a situation, all the facts are never available to us, for much of the relevant material is inaccessible to any one of us. I cannot judge you because I don't know all the factors that enter into your decisions or your actions.

In the beginning of the verse in James, he reminds his readers that "There is one Lawgiver, who is able to save and to destroy" (4:12*a*). The Lawgiver is the Judge, the one who can pronounce freedom or punishment. There is only one Judge, because there is only One who can infallibly know the heart of the matter. James says also, "Do not grumble against one another, brethren, lest you be condemned. Behold, the Judge is standing at the door!" (5:9). God is He who looks upon the hearts of human beings and cuts through to intentions.

It's mighty inconvenient for us that He has the ability to see right into our hearts. Have you seen those lead bags that film is put into to protect it from airport X-rays? Well, sometimes I would like to have some spiritually similar apparatus so that the eyes of God could not see through to my heart! But that's impossible. He not only knows, He understands.

In the Episcopal tradition, we begin our service of Holy Communion by reminding ourselves that this is the kind of God we have: "Almighty God, unto whom all hearts are open, all desires known, and from whom no secrets are hid. . . ." Our God can penetrate into the heart of each one of us and give a right judgment every time. He stands as judge over us if we judge another! This means that when we are disposed to criticize one another harshly, God takes note not only of what we are saying, but also of who is doing the criticizing.

Jesus warned against this, saying "Judge not, and you shall not be judged. Condemn not, and you shall not be condemned. Forgive, and you will be forgiven" (Luke 6:37). If ever there were a reason not to judge another, that is it! If we don't judge others, God will not judge us. If we really believed that, I wonder how much of our talking about one another and negotiation against one another would go on? It isn't a question of being right—what we say may well be a true assessment of the situation. But even if it's right, it's still judgment; and the question is, who are we to judge?

Vertical and Horizontal

This is a very clear example of something we find in Scripture: that our relationship to God and what we gain from Him is in direct relationship to the way we relate to one another. The church by and large has wanted to forget that through the ages. We have liked believing that somehow we could cultivate our own spirituality—you know, "Just You and me, God, gradually developing me into a spiritual giant!" We do all this without any reference to being united to others. This "Lone Ranger" approach to Christianity is totally foreign to Scripture. (It was also foreign to the Lone Ranger—he had Tonto!)

All the way through Scripture, we are told that if we say we love God and are in disunity with those around us, we are lying. God has made it very clear that there is no possibility of our being in a right relationship with Him and in a wrong relationship with others.

I'm not advocating peaceful relationships because that would be nice. What I am saying is that our relationship to God is never stronger than our horizontal relationship with others. Husbands and wives, parents and children need to know that, because in the process of living together it's easy to allow small strains to creep into relationships. Churches need to know that because it's easy, even in a well-intentioned congregation, for resentments to build into high, thick walls of separation. Communities need to know that because misunderstandings can generate poor cooperation. Countries need to know that because hostilities can develop into wars. Try as we can to divorce the two, we cannot put asunder what God has joined. We can't have external relationships that are stronger than our relationship with God, and we can't have a strong relationship with God unless we have strong relationships with others.

How do we strengthen those relationships that are in need of mending? Well, for starters, Jesus said that if we forgive, we will be forgiven. That's what we say in the Lord's prayer: "Forgive us our sins as we forgive those who sin against us." Our receiving forgiveness is wholly contingent upon our giving it, no matter how wounded we are. God is saying that if we are unable to gain harmony on the horizontal plane with those whom we see, what makes us think we can have harmony with a God we cannot see?

Jesus said, "Give, and it will be given to you: good measure, pressed down, shaken together, and running over will be put into your bosom. For with the same measure that you use, it will be measured back to you" (Luke 6:38). That is a summary statement for the whole paragraph. The measure that you and I use to judge each other is the measure by which we will be judged. The measure with which we condemn, we will be condemned. The measure with which we forgive, we will be forgiven. Jesus is not talking about salvation here; He is talking about the practical, everyday relationships being worked out with each other and with Him. The measure that we give to the relationship is exactly and precisely the measure that we will get back. The degree with which we harbor resentments and hatred is the same degree to which we remove ourselves from the forgiveness we are offered by God.

One thing that gets in the way of fence-mending is that if we decide the fence looks too far gone, we had better plan on getting a new one. You know how it is—the relationship is so broken that it would be painful to go back to try to right it again, and it probably wouldn't work, anyway. But Jesus says we should not judge something according to appearance, but rather with righteous judgment. Don't look at the outside. Be obedient! Be willing to risk! Only God knows the heart of the situation, and if you are obedient to Him and offer the situation to Him, you will be able to gain some good.

In Genesis 18 there is a wonderful little statement about God, "Shall not the Judge of all the earth do right?" (v. 25). His judgment is the completely righteous one; ours is totally flawed. Only He knows why people act the way they do, why there is separation between churches and communities and countries. Only He knows the way to Peace—He is our Peace.

Let me give you an example. It is no great Christian virtue that I don't often lose my temper. I'm jut not inclined to do so. It isn't due to any degree of self-control; there simply isn't a struggle. I would tend to say "who cares?" and walk away from a situation before I would blow up. For others, however, temper is a terrible test. In God's sight they might have accomplished more progress in that area through struggle and submission than I would in a lifetime. But people would not know that from my outward appearance. That's why judgments are so erroneous—they are limited to what we see. So in mending fences it's important that we go into the mending with no preconceived expectations of the outcome, no prejudgments. Be totally open to the leading of the Holy Spirit.

Judged by Our Standards

Romans 2 reminds us of another problem with judgment, one that has been often observed by psychologists. People tend to judge others by what they do themselves. We may notice that what drives us up a wall about someone is something with which we struggle ourselves. There are certain things that I have not wanted my children to do, and when I examined them, I found they were the very things I liked least about myself. There are some ways in which the resemblance of children to parents is not a compliment! They can imitate us, but most often they pick up our worst characteristics.

Jesus told us to remove the log in our own eye before we try to remove the speck in another's. Paul elaborates in Romans:

> Therefore you are inexcusable, O man, whoever you are who judge, for in whatever you judge another you condemn yourself; for you who judge practice the same things. But we know that the judgment of God is according to truth against those who practice such things. And do you think this, O man, you who judge those practicing such things, and doing the same, that you will escape the judgment of God? (2:1–3).

Scripture makes it clear that when we pass out judgment we judge ourselves. In Romans 14 we find one of the most offensive areas in judging one another. Somehow we believe (although we seldom articulate it) that our standards ought to be those by which the world is to be measured. A priest once said to me, "My opinions are convictions, while yours are prejudices!" Our opinions represent the truth; our values are sterling and supreme. We don't say it, because we know it's ludicrous, but we do act that way toward one another. Well, don't we? Be honest! But Paul kind of cuts to the core:

"Receive one who is weak in the faith, but not to disputes over doubtful things" (v. 1). Don't argue with people who have different opinions than yours! Resist the tendency to try to correct everyone. After all, we are constantly growing, and may understand something tomorrow that we did not understand yesterday! "For one believes he may eat all things, but he who is weak eats only vegetables" (v. 2). My daughter Andrea is a vegetarian, and I am not about to try to correct her by telling her that the Bible says she is weak. That would not strengthen our relationship at all!

But more than that, Paul goes on to say, "Let not him who eats despise him who does not eat, and let him who does not eat judge him who eats, for God has received him. Who are you to judge another's servant?" (vv. 3–4*a*). God Himself is the judge, and people are accountable only to Him, not to us. They are His servants. "To his own master he stands or falls. Indeed, he will be made to stand, for God is able to make him stand" (v. 4*b*). Each one of us answers to God in our own way for our obedience to the way He has led us.

"One person esteems one day above another; another esteems every day alike. Let each be convinced in his own mind" (v. 5). It's all right to be committed to a particular tradition, but only for ourselves. We should not seek to impose our beliefs on everyone else. We should allow others the liberty we would like to have ourselves in the Lord. "He who observes the day, observes it to the Lord; and he who does not observe the day, to the Lord he does not observe it. He who eats, eats to the Lord, for he gives God thanks; and he who does not eat, to the Lord he does not eat, and gives God thanks" (v. 6).

And then the heart of the matter: "For none of us lives to himself, and no one dies to himself. For if we live, we live to the Lord; and if we die, we die to the Lord. Therefore, whether we live or die, we are the Lord's. For to this end Christ died and rose and lived again, that He might be Lord of both the dead and the living" (vv. 7–9). Our relationship with God is reflected in our relationship to others; ultimately, we belong to God.

Paul is discussing the proper attitude Christians are to have toward one another in debatable areas of conduct. There are some things that are not debatable! Doctrinal issues of faith are not debatable, although you'd hardly realize that in these times. Some persons spend their time trying to undo all that Christ has done. But even when we come across those whose actions seek to suck the very life's blood from Christianity, we must bear in mind that we are not to judge them. "But why do you judge your brother? Or why do you show contempt for your brother? For we shall all stand before the judgment seat of Christ. For it is written: 'As I live, says the LORD, every knee shall bow to Me, and every tongue shall confess to God.' So then each of us shall give account of himself to God" (vv. 10–12).

Ultimately, whether the issue is minor or major, we will appear before the judgment seat of God. This is a sobering thought. This judgment does not refer to salvation—Scripture is very clear that if we have come to Christ and have accepted Him as our Savior, the matter of our ultimate salvation is forever settled. The judgment seat is not to determine whether or not we will make it! We will be judged in reference to what we have done with what we have been given—the way we have lived our lives, our faithfulness to our faith, and the attitudes with which we react to one another.

Grace is available to us that allows us to allow others to be themselves. The Holy Spirit will work that quality into our lives, and we will begin to lose the compulsions that cause us to leap to judgment, little by little. Have you ever thought how dull the world would be if it were populated only by people like us?

Accepting Differences

Paul goes on to exhort: "Therefore let us not judge one another anymore, but rather resolve this, not to put a stumbling block or a cause to fall in our brother's way" (v. 13). There is something about an argument over faith that produces unbelief rather than faith in a person. I have known many more people who have been loved into the kingdom than who have been convinced into it! Let the witness you give be loving and persuasive, not hostile, or you will build a barrier between the Lord and the person.

"Do you have faith? Have it to yourself before God. Happy is he who does not condemn himself in what he approves" (v. 22).

Paul is not here defending "private" religion. ("My belief is just between me and God, thank you.") He is saying that the way God leads us is ours, and is unique to us—it can't be cloned. If the Lord is leading you to some particular spiritual devotion, that is business conducted between you and Him. Exercise that ministry to Him. If, for instance, you are led to fast on Fridays, don't try to make it a group effort! In giving a testimony, don't try to lead others to follow the way God has led you. That attitude denies the unique individuality of each one's spiritual walk.

We have to deal with the basic attitudes we have toward one another if we are going to satisfy our thirst for unity. We are going to have to accept each other as we are, for who we are, allowing for differences, and refuse to enter into criticism of one another. We must do this because we recognize that we stand and fall before God alone; no one has to measure up to our standards. And we need to remember that we will, in fact, be measured by the measures we use.

Not long ago I was privileged to witness the testimony given by many people to a man who had died suddenly and tragically in the prime of his life. He was not a man of influence in the world's terms. He didn't hold an important position; he wasn't a man of great education or riches. But hundreds of people mourned his loss, and one of the most frequent things they shared about him was that they had never heard him say an unkind word about anyone, ever! Some had known him for thirty or forty years, had been with him on a regular basis, but had never heard him utter a word of judgment. Miraculous—in this day and age, a man who spread love and acceptance as naturally as he breathed. The fruits of the Spirit blossomed in that man for all to share; there was no machete of judgment to cut them down at the roots. On the day when that man appears before the Lord, he will hear: "Well done." And because of his witness, many others will try to emulate his life and seek the source of his strength.

Wheat and Tares

I want to examine one last area, one Jesus raised in his parable of the wheat and tares. You will recall that a man sowed wheat in a field and his servant came to him, saying that there were tares, which are weeds, growing in the field along with the wheat. Should he weed them out? But the owner replied, "No, lest while you gather up the tares you also uproot the wheat with them. Let both grow together until the harvest, and at the time of harvest I will say to the reapers,

'First gather together the tares and bind them in bundles to burn them, but gather the wheat into my barn'" (Matt. 13:29–30).

This is one of the few parables Jesus interpreted Himself.

> Then Jesus sent the multitude away and went into the house. And His disciples came to Him, saying, "Explain to us the parable of the tares of the field." He answered and said to them, "He who sows the good seed is the Son of Man. The field is the world, the good seeds are the sons of the kingdom, but the tares are the sons of the wicked one. The enemy who sowed them is the devil, the harvest is the end of the age, and the reapers are the angels. Therefore as the tares are gathered and burned in the fire, so it will be at the end of this age. The Son of Man will send out His angels, and they will gather out of His kingdom all things that offend, and those who practice lawlessness, and will cast them into the furnace of fire. There will be wailing and gnashing of teeth. Then the righteous will shine forth as the sun in the kingdom of their Father. He who has ears to hear, let him hear!" (Matt. 13:36–43).

The field is the world. The wheat is God's people, the tares are the children of the evil one. Do you remember what the servant said to the householder? "Should we weed the garden?" In other words, is it our job to go out and try to separate the wheat from the tares, to try to gather a little pure fellowship of wheat in which there are no weeds? The answer was "No." Why? Because you might include wheat, thinking it to be tares. In other words, you simply do not have the knowledge upon which to make that judgment.

Sometimes I shudder at the way people speak of others, willingly consigning them to the pit of hell, saying this one is a believer and that one isn't. That kind of judgment is based on artificial and superficial discernment at best! Often we want to know the minute the person encountered Christ, or said the sinner's prayer, or some other standard by which we could measure their spirituality. But it is not up to us to measure their spirituality! We have no basis, no way to make that kind of judgment, and here Jesus expressly forbids it. Sometimes people think whole other churches are filled with unbelievers. How can they say that? Where did they gain such omniscience?

Jesus gave us His guidance for discerning the spiritual life of others.

> You will know them by their fruits. Do men gather grapes from thornbushes or figs from thistles? Even so, every good tree bears good fruit, but a bad tree bears bad fruit. A good tree cannot bear

bad fruit, nor can a bad tree bear good fruit. Every tree that does not bear good fruit is cut down and thrown into the fire. Therefore, by their fruits you will know them (Matt. 7:16–17).

We are not to judge—God does that. But we are permitted to inspect the fruit of their lives. First, though, ask yourself: Does the fruit of the Spirit blossom in your life? Because if you are manifesting love, joy, peace, longsuffering, kindness, goodness, faithfulness, gentleness, and self-control, judgment will not flow from you. It is as simple as that.

Proper Judgment

God does not mean that we are to gather into little "holy huddles" and separate ourselves from everyone else. We will never be able to form an enclave of perfectly pure people! It is not the will of God for us to separate from the world, because God loves the people of the world and Christ came to save them. But we are given guidance to avoid some people.

The apostle Paul wrote a letter to the Corinthians that has not survived. There was a letter written prior to what we know as the "first letter to the Corinthians." We know about it because Paul refers to it in other letters. One thing Paul evidently said in the missing letter was not to fellowship with people who were doing all sorts of evil things. But they didn't understand his direction, and apparently, in a letter he received from them, expressed their misunderstanding of his teaching. So he wrote to correct the impression he had given.

> I wrote to you in my epistle not to keep company with sexually immoral people. Yet I certainly did not mean with the sexually immoral people of this world, or with the covetous, or extortioners, or idolaters, since then you would need to go out of the world. But now I have written to you not to keep company with anyone named a brother, who is sexually immoral, or covetous, or an idolater, or a reviler, or a drunkard, or an extortioner—not even to eat with such a person. For what have I to do with judging those who are outside? Do you not judge those who are inside? But those who are outside God judges. Therefore "put away from yourselves the evil person" (1 Cor. 5:9–13).

There is a place for judgment within the Church, for those who claim to be Christians. There is a standard of life we can rightfully expect from one another, and if we have a professing Christian who is living in open violation of that standard, he or she will bring discredit and dishonor on the church. We are not to fellowship with that person. The Book of Common Prayer says exactly the same thing. An instruction to the priest in the service of Holy Communion says that if "a person who is living a notoriously evil life" comes to the altar, he is to be turned away. You might be shocked at that, but the instruction does not refer to just any sinner. It's not a person with a difficult problem, say an alcoholic who is struggling. This means a person who is a professing Christian but who is living in open and unrepentant violation of the commandments of God. There comes a time in the life of the church when, in order to maintain the welfare of the church, discipline must be exercised. But we are to be very clear that we have all the facts.

Some years ago I had occasion to refuse Communion to a man who was openly living in an adulterous relationship. I had warned my assistant to meet him at the door of the church and tell him I would not give the sacraments to him.

He was furious! But in the end, he repented, was reconciled to his wife, and I performed their second wedding to each other. Would that reconciliation have happened if I had looked the other way and allowed him to partake of the sacraments? What we are told is that if a person receives the sacraments unworthily, he brings judgment upon himself. So there is good reason to exercise limited judgment within the confines of the church.

The unity we seek is possible only in a non-judgmental atmosphere. Consider this chapter carefully. Ponder the words of Scripture, examine your heart. Allow the Lord to make you into a person known for compassion, love, winsomeness, and understanding.

Ask Him to take from you the natural tendency to evaluate others according to your standards, to judge others who don't measure up. Stop trying to correct the whole world. It's not ours to correct! God alone will bring about the unity we desire if we will get out of His way, and stop building stumbling blocks of judgment in the way of others.

PRAYER

Grant, O God, that your holy and life-giving Spirit may so move every human heart, that barriers which divide us may crumble, suspicions disappear, and hatreds cease; that our divisions being healed, we may live in justice and peace; through Jesus Christ our Lord. Amen.   —Prayer for Social Justice

— QUESTIONS —

Have you ever been the victim of someone's judgment? How did you feel?

Would you say that the vertical relationship you have with God is reflected in the horizontal relationships you have with others?

How many fences do you need to mend?

If you were judged by God using the standard you use for others, how would you fare before His throne?

CHAPTER 10

Thirsting for Integrity

A FEW WEEKS AGO I encountered a woman who was holding a magazine in her hand and becoming more and more upset as she read an article in it. She finally threw it down on the table and said, "What nerve! That man calls himself a Christian and has involved himself with a number of women at once, impregnating two of them and then marrying another! What kind of heroes are there for our kids to emulate today?"

Her anger echoes a question asked in the media many times over the years—what has happened to our role models? What ever happened to integrity? This country, this culture, this world, thirsts for integrity. Does anybody really know what the word means anymore?

Integrity means whole, of a piece, unbroken, or complete. It means honesty, sincerity, uprightness; it means soundness, dependability. What had so upset the woman with the magazine article was that the person was saying one thing with his mouth and proclaiming yet another by his actions. There was nothing dependable about his witness. Because this person was a well-known sports figure, his example would be there before many impressionable young boys. How many would, in later years, think it was perfectly all right to do as this sports star had done?

What upset her the most was that he had proclaimed himself a Christian. Like it or not, there is an expectation that when a person comes to Christ, the quality of his or her life will be different. Falling back into the rut of the world's way of living is to miss out on what God has for us.

Extraordinary Living

The apostle Paul makes a point of this expectation in the second chapter of his letter of the Colossians.

Therefore, if you died with Christ from the basic principles of the world, why, as though living in the world, do you subject yourselves to regulations— . . . according to the commandments and doctrines of men? These things indeed have an appearance of wisdom in self-imposed religion, false humility, and neglect of the body, but are of no value against the indulgence of the flesh (vv. 20, 22–23*b*).

In the earlier chapters of Paul's letter to the Corinthians, he complains that they are living and acting as ordinary people. "Well, what's wrong with that?" you might ask. "Weren't they just ordinary people?" The trouble is that when we come to the Lord, He expects to see an extraordinary quality in our lives. The interesting thing about Paul's question to the Colossians is that it discusses worldly living. Worldly living as described on the pages of Scripture is not worldly living as it is thought of by many people. Paul asks, "Why do you live as if you still belonged to the world? Why do you submit to its rules?"

Earlier in this chapter, Paul has written that we come to fullness of life through our relationship with Jesus Christ.

As you therefore have received Christ Jesus the Lord, so walk in Him, rooted and built up in Him and established in the faith, as you have been taught, abounding in it with thanksgiving. Beware lest anyone cheat you through philosophy and empty deceit, according to the tradition of men, according to the basic principles of the world, and not according to Christ. For in Him dwells all the fullness of the Godhead bodily; and you are complete in Him, who is the head of all principality and power (vv. 6–10).

Jesus is God incarnate, and in Him we are complete. Jesus promised that we would have life, and have it abundantly. Abundantly and completely—all we need comes from our relationship to Christ; particularly, all we need to overcome the sins of the flesh.

In Him you were also circumcised with the circumcision made without hands, by putting off the body of the sins of the flesh, by the circumcision of Christ, buried with Him in baptism, in which you also were raised with Him through faith in the working of God, who raised Him from the dead. And you, being dead in your trespasses and the uncircumcision of your flesh, He has made alive together with Him, having forgiven you all trespasses (vv. 11–13).

When Jesus died on the cross, it was, in the mind of God, as though we died with Him. When He was raised from the dead, it was as though we were raised with Him. In other words, we have been identified with Jesus in His death, and we are to be identified with Him in His new life and resurrection power. All our sins are forgiven.

The next verses go on to say that God nailed the debt that we owed to the cross: "Having wiped out the handwriting of requirements that was against us, which was contrary to us. And He has taken it out of the way, having nailed it to the cross. Having disarmed principalities and powers, He made a public spectacle of them, triumphing over them in it" (vv. 14–15).

Today, with all of the press and publicity that Satan is given, this truth needs to be proclaimed! Somehow our society does not seem to realize that our God, through the resurrection of His Son Jesus Christ, has triumphed over the forces of evil. This is the purpose for which He came—to destroy the works of the evil one. Here we are told that He made a public spectacle of His triumph over them. Why haven't we noticed?

We bear some responsibility for this. Paul goes on to warn:

Let no one cheat you of your reward, taking delight in false humility and worship of angels, intruding into those things which he has not seen, vainly puffed up by his fleshly mind, and not holding fast to the Head, from whom all the body, nourished and knit together by joints and ligaments, grows with the increase that is from God (vv. 18–19).

Watch Out!

There are things to watch out for, or we will miss out on God's best for us. Take false humility, for instance. A whole area of Christian teaching today puts a tremendous emphasis on constantly crucifying ourselves. That is not what the Bible teaches. We are crucified with Christ, but our crucifixion is not suicide. It is not something we can do ourselves. Think about it in literal terms: at most we might be able to hammer the nails into our feet and perhaps one hand—then what? We are crucified with Christ as the Spirit of God does the work of putting to death in us those things that are contrary to the purpose and plan of God. We are to BE crucified.

Self-abasement is false humility and not the product of the Spirit at all, which is what the rest of the verses mean. This happens when a person has lost connection with the Head, that is, Jesus. It is Jesus who supports and holds together the body and causes it to grow. Staying connected to Jesus enables the life of God to purify us and to work in us, so that the life we live is in line with the belief we proclaim. The integrity of the gospel message is proclaimed in word and deed.

I live in New England, and in the fall of the year, most of the leaves on the trees turn various colors and fall from the trees. I have always noticed that lots of dead leaves cling to the trees throughout the winter. I suppose that if I were troubled by that, I could go out with a ladder and climb up and pull them off the branches, one by one. That's rather compulsive behavior, but it could be done.

But I have noticed that if I wait until springtime, when new life begins to come into the trees, then the old, dead leaves simply drop away. That's what Paul is talking about. God purifies us. We are dealing with the Holy Spirit dwelling within us, and as He is used in more and more of our lives, then those things that are contrary to the Lord will fall away. The strange thing is, if we attack our sins with vigor, we will only become obsessed with them, much like tearing the leaves from the tree. Integrity cannot be accomplished by trying to live sinless lives. It is only available through the exercise of spiritual grace within us.

Why?

Paul still asks, "Why do you live as though you still belonged to the world?" What does he mean? In Galatians 4 we find this statement: "But then, indeed, when you did not know God, you served those which by nature are not gods. But now after you have known God, or rather are known by God, how is it that you turn again to the weak and beggarly elements, to which you desire again to be in bondage?" (vv. 8–9).

A few chapters back I quoted Paul Tillich's belief that your god was whatever ultimately concerned you. This is essentially what Paul is saying here—you served those that by nature are not gods. Now that you know God, or rather God knows you and counts you as one of His people, why do you turn again to those things that will put you in bondage?

The opposite of integrity in hypocrisy. Jesus points out the essence of hypocrisy in his words to the Pharisees: "Well did Isaiah prophesy of you hypocrites, as it is written: 'This people honors Me with their lips, but their heart is far from Me'" (Mark 7:6).

Giving only lip service to God is hypocrisy. Jesus further elaborated on this: "What comes out of a man, that defiles a man. For from within, out of the heart of men, proceed evil thoughts, adulteries, fornications, murders, thefts, covetousness, wickedness, deceit, lewdness, an evil eye, blasphemy, pride, foolishness. All these evil things come from within and defile a man" (Mark 7:20–23).

Unless our hearts are submitted to the Lord, our proclamations of faith are useless! We can sit in church week after week, receive the sacraments, and work hard on the committees. But if our hearts are not submitted to Christ, if they harbor a secret life of sin, there is no integrity to our faith.

Matthew records Jesus' words to the Pharisees: "Woe to you, scribes and Pharisees, hypocrites! For you are like whitewashed tombs which indeed appear beautiful outwardly, but inside are full of dead men's bones and all uncleanness. Even so you also outwardly appear righteous to men, but inside you are full of hypocrisy and lawlessness" (Matt. 23:27–28).

These are very somber words. These are the words for which Jesus was crucified. There is no question about it: Jesus angered the religious leaders of his day because he called into question the whole matter of their integrity!

We need to learn to trust and submit to the Lord completely. When the Spirit of God has full reign in our lives, then we won't have to worry about integrity. When we call ourselves Christians, that label carries with it the image of Christ. Are we worthy of the Name?

God's will has not changed. We change when we yield to the Spirit of God. We change from the inside out, and our desire is to do what God wants. The outward working of our lives will be in harmony with the inner working of our spirits, as an expression of our new life in Christ. Then integrity will become as natural as breathing.

PRAYER

Almighty and merciful God, it is only by your gift that your faithful people offer you true and laudable service: Grant that we may run without stumbling to obtain your heavenly promises; through Jesus Christ our Lord, who lives and reigns with you and the Holy Spirit, one God, now and for ever. Amen.

—Proper 26

— QUESTIONS —

Do your words and actions match?

What worldly attitudes do you still embrace?

What would you like to nail to Jesus' cross right now?

CHAPTER 11

Thirsting for Truth

FOR MANY YEARS, I was a student of philosophy. I loved the various schools of thought and reasoning. I even taught logic and ethics for a time.

Two areas of philosophy come most into play in the life of a Christian: metaphysics and epistemology. Metaphysics is the search for the ultimate—to understand the all-inclusive plan of the world and the part we play in it. Epistemology deals with what we know—Do we really know anything, and if so, what? How do we know that we know it? And, if we take that idea a bit further, how do we know that we know that we know it?

These questions form the human thirst for truth. What is truth? How do we know it's true? And how do we know that we know it's true? Jesus answered the question about truth two thousand years ago. He said, "I am the way, the truth, and the life" (John 14:6). Ever since He walked the earth, people have been asking, "Do we really know that? How do we know that? How do we know that we know that?" Let's look at the truth about the Truth.

In Matthew 22, we find a number of questions that are asked by the Pharisees of Jesus. They are asked in a hostile atmosphere. "Then the Pharisees went and plotted how they might entangle Him in His talk" (v. 15). They sought to expose Jesus, to bring Him into disfavor with the people. They thought the best method to use was to ask Him questions, the answers to which would not please the people. These were carefully calculated questions, asked not out of a desire to know the answer. They were seeking to entangle Him in His talk, to discredit Him. They "set Him up," so to speak: "And they sent to Him their disciples with the Herodians, saying, 'Teacher, we know that You are true, and teach the way of God in truth; nor do You care about anyone, for You do not regard the person of men'" (v. 16).

Political Power

The Pharisees and the Herodians were two of three principal groups within the land at that time. The Pharisees were a religious sect, conservatives among the people of Israel. They favored the law of Moses and the oral tradition. They emphasized that it was important to understand not only the law, but also the Talmud, or the rabbinical interpretations of the law that had gradually developed over the centuries. They believed that the law of Moses, with its 613 commandments, covered virtually every area of life. The rabbis then took those laws (as found in the first five books of Moses) and refined them, enlarged upon them, and gave anecdotes to illustrate them, in an attempt to cover every conceivable experience that could arise in life.

When you read about the scribes, or lawyers, with the Pharisees, you are reading about people who were interested in these refinements of the law. The Pharisees were dedicated to keeping every work of the law to the very last detail—they were concerned that the washing of hands be done in a precise way, for instance. These were the keepers of the law and its interpretation, and they were a considerable force of power in Jesus' day.

The Herodians were the political opportunists of the day. Herod was king, and Herod's sons were, at the time these words were written, seated on various thrones throughout the land. The Herodians were the people who supported the ruling establishment. Herod, as king, was despised by the Jews, particularly because he was a half-breed; he was partly Edomite. The Herodians, then, were those Jewish people who went along with the political establishment.

Normally, the Pharisees and the Herodians would have nothing in common with each other. They were not usually on speaking terms; but in this case, they were united in their opposition to Jesus.

If we go a bit further along in this chapter, we will find the appearance of yet another party: the Sadducees. "The same day the Sadducees, who say there is no resurrection, came to Him and asked Him . . ." (v. 23). The Sadducees were the liberal religious party of the day, and they were the dominant group. Most of the seats on the Jewish Sanhedrin, the ruling council of seventy Jews, were taken by

Sadducees. They believed only in the law of Moses. They did not hold to the oral tradition or to the rabbinic tradition, so they were not nearly as concerned with minor details as the Pharisees were. They did not believe in the resurrection of the dead. They normally had nothing to do with the other sects, except for the fact that they were against Jesus.

The Questions

The Pharisees and Herodians raised their question after they had paved the way with a bit of flattery. "Teacher, we know that You are true, . . . Tell us therefore, what do You think? Is it lawful to pay taxes to Caesar, or not?" (Matt. 22:16–17). They didn't care what the answer was. They wanted Him to take a stand that would alienate the crowd. If Jesus said it was lawful to pay taxes to Caesar, a lot of the people would be angry because Rome was occupying their land and the Romans were hated by the Jews. To give an affirmative answer would be encouraging the Jews to remain subservient to the powers of Rome.

On the other hand, to give a negative reply would bring Jesus into conflict with the Roman state and therefore make Him liable to be arrested. Either way He answered, He would encounter trouble.

But Jesus perceived their wickedness, and said, "Why do you test Me, you hypocrites? Show Me the tax money." So they brought him a denarius. And He said to them, "Whose image and inscription is this?" They said to Him, "Caesar's." And He said to them, "Render therefore to Caesar the things that are Caesar's, and to God the things that are God's" (vv. 18–21).

It didn't work. He didn't fall for their trap. What's more, He didn't give them an answer they could argue about! They were mystified. Then the Sadducees confronted Jesus:

Teacher, Moses said that if a man dies, having no children, his brother shall marry his wife and raise up offspring for his brother. Now there were with us seven brothers. The first died after he had married, and having no offspring, left his wife to his brother. Likewise the second also, and the third, even to the seventh. Last of all the woman died also. Therefore, in the resurrection, whose wife of the seven will she be? For they all had her (vv. 24–28).

Bear in mind that these men didn't believe in the resurrection, so the question was meaningless to them. They were simply hoping to embarrass Jesus. Jesus answered that question by saying:

"You are mistaken, not knowing the Scriptures nor the power of God. For in the resurrection they neither marry nor are given in marriage, but are like angels of God in heaven. But concerning the resurrection of the dead, have you not read what was spoken to you by God, saying, 'I am the God of Abraham, the God of Isaac, and the God of Jacob'? God is not the God of the dead, but of the living" (vv. 29–32).

Jesus, in answering, pointed out that they didn't know what they thought they knew. The case cited was immaterial, because life after death is rooted in the character of God. Abraham, Isaac, and Jacob were dead to the world but alive to God; He still identified Himself with them. The Sadducees were stopped in their tracks.

Jesus' Question

Then it was Jesus' turn to ask a question.

While the Pharisees were gathered together, Jesus asked them, say-ing, "What do you think about the Christ? Whose Son is He?" They said to Him, "The Son of David." He said to them, "How then does David in the Spirit call Him 'Lord,' saying:
  'The LORD said to my Lord,
 "Sit at My right hand,
   Till I make Your enemies Your footstool" '?
   If David then calls Him 'Lord,' how is He his Son?" And no one was able to answer Him a word, nor from that day on did anyone dare question Him anymore (vv. 41–46).

I want to concentrate on the first part of Jesus' question. "What do you think about the Christ? Whose Son is He?" We are familiar with the use of the term *Christ*. Christ is not a name; it is a title. In the Old Testament, there are prophetic words about a coming Messiah. The Hebrew word translated *Messiah* is the word meaning "Anointed One." Many were anointed in the Old Testament—prophets, priests, kings, judges—but there is an understanding of one specially anointed servant, who began to be called "Messiah." In the Greek language in which the New Testament was written, the word for "Anointed One" is *Christos*. When we say "Christ" we are saying "Anointed One."

When we say we believe in Jesus Christ, we are saying we believe that Jesus is the Anointed One, the prophesied Messiah.

So Jesus asked the question, "What do you think about the Christ (or the Messiah)? Whose Son is He?" He was not asking a question about Himself, because the Pharisees were not prepared to admit that He was the Messiah. He was just asking them what they believed; and then He asked them how they knew what they thought they knew. "How is it, then, that if the Messiah is the Son of David, that David calls Him Lord?"

The Son of David

Why was that idea so important? Why did the Pharisees say, "The Son of David"? If we go back into the Old Testament Scriptures, we will find that the promised Messiah was indeed to be a descendant of David. God's promise to David is recorded in 1 Chronicles:

> "And it shall be, when your days are fulfilled, when you must go to be with your fathers, that I will set up your seed after you, who will be one of your sons; that I will establish his kingdom. He shall build Me a house, and I will establish his throne forever. I will be his Father, and he shall be My son, and I will not take My mercy away from him, as I took it from him who was before you. And I will establish him in My house and in My kingdom forever; and his throne shall be established forever" (1 Chron. 17:11-14).

Those who know biblical history will know that the first part of this promise was literally fulfilled in David's son, Solomon. Solomon succeeded David on the throne of Israel and built a great temple in Jerusalem—a house for God, so to speak.

If we read the passage carefully, we will discover statements that seem to be more than could be fulfilled by a mere human being. Solomon's throne was not an eternal throne. God was not Solomon's Father. That would have been a strange way for God to speak. If you stretched the point, you could say that Solomon, as a descendant of Abraham, was a child of God, but that would not account for the intimate relationship of a Father and Son to which God was referring. True, God is spoken of as "Father" in the Old Testament, but in the collective sense, much as He is spoken of as "husband" to His people. Here God is saying, "David, I will be his Father, and he will be My son. I will not take My love from him, as I did with Saul." God was with Saul at first, but little by little his heart turned from the

Lord, until finally the Lord rejected him as king. Scripture says "He took away from him His steadfast love." Here God promises David that He will never take away His steadfast love from this son of David, but will confirm him in God's house and kingdom and give him an eternal throne. The house of the Lord was the temple. This Son was to occupy a special place in the temple as the great high priest, and sit on the throne as king.

Judah's Line

This is not the first time these messianic prophecies speaking of the coming One suggest that there was to be a king among the descendants of Abraham. If we go back to the book of Genesis, we will find that the original covenant made with Abraham nearly two thousand years before Christ was renewed with Abraham's son, Isaac, and then with Isaac's son, Jacob. Jacob was the father of twelve sons, who became in turn the fathers of the twelve tribes of Israel. Before he died, Jacob imparted a patriarchal blessing to his sons. This is what he said to his son Judah, perhaps sixteen or seventeen hundred years before Jesus was born: "The scepter shall not depart from Judah, nor a lawgiver from between his feet, until Shiloh comes; and to Him shall be the obedience of the people" (Gen. 49:10). A scepter is a symbol of kingly power, and Jacob was saying that the scepter would not depart from Judah's inheritance until it came to Shiloh. Shiloh means "the One who brings Peace." The Messiah, therefore, would be of the tribe of Judah, bringing a kingship of peace.

Let's skip down the line of Judah a few generations. Isaiah wrote the following prophecy eight centuries before Jesus' birth:

> There shall come forth a Rod from the stem of Jesse,
> And a Branch shall grow out of his roots.
> The Spirit of the LORD shall rest upon Him,
> The Spirit of wisdom and understanding,
> The Spirit of counsel and might,
> The Spirit of knowledge and of the fear of the LORD.
> His delight is in the fear of the LORD,
> And He shall not judge by the sight of His eyes,
> Nor decide by the hearing of His ears;
> But with righteousness He shall judge the poor,
> And decide with equity for the meek of the earth;
> He shall strike the earth with the rod of His mouth,
> And with the breath of His lips He shall slay the wicked.

> Righteousness shall be the belt of His loins,
> And faithfulness the belt of His waist (Isa. 11:1–5).

Jesse was the father of David, the king whose son would reign forever. Jesse came from Bethlehem. The family tree of David would be felled, but here God is saying that from the stem, or stump, a Rod, or shoot, would grow in the person of the Messiah—a Branch from the roots of Jesse. He would be characterized by the fullness of the Holy Spirit of God, and absolute integrity.

Let's go to Jeremiah for further illumination: " 'Behold, the days are coming,' says the LORD, 'that I will raise to David a Branch of righteousness; a King shall reign and prosper, and execute judgment and righteousness in the earth. In His days Judah will be saved, and Israel will dwell safely; now this is His name by which He will be called: THE LORD OUR RIGHTEOUSNESS' " (Jer. 23:5–6).

The Lord spoke to Jeremiah six hundred years before Jesus' birth. By then, David had been dead for four hundred years, and yet God reiterated His promise to David that there would one day be a descendant of his upon a throne. The stem of Isaiah has become the Branch, who shall reign as king. But this king is no ordinary king. He will be called THE LORD OUR RIGHTEOUSNESS.

In Micah 5:2 we find a passage that is so familiar we almost take it for granted: "But you, Bethlehem Ephrathah, though you are little among the thousands of Judah, yet out of you shall come forth to Me the One to be Ruler in Israel, whose goings forth are from of old, from everlasting."

Bethlehem Ephrathah was the ancient name for Bethlehem, Bethlehem meaning "house of bread" and Ephrathah meaning "fruitful." This was the birthplace of David. Micah was a contemporary of Isaiah, speaking eight hundred years before Jesus' birth. He prophesied that from the small village of Bethlehem would come a ruler whose origin was from old, from everlasting.

Do you see the biblical basis that led the Pharisees to answer "The Son of David" to Jesus' question, "Whose Son is the Christ?" These passages would have told them how they knew what they knew to be true. The Son of David, the Branch from the stem of Jesse, would be the Christ, the Messiah, the Anointed One.

Mighty God

Another prophetic verse found in Isaiah is familiar to us all. "For unto us a Child is born, unto us a Son is given; and the government will be upon His shoulder. And His name will be called Wonderful, Counselor, Mighty God, Everlasting Father, Prince of Peace" (Isa. 9:6).

The verse starts off rather ordinarily—unto us a Child is born; unto us a Son is given. As wonderful as the birth of a child is, it is not an extraordinary event—of all the children that are born, roughly half of them are sons. Then Isaiah says that the government will be upon His shoulder. Other children have been born heirs to thrones from the moment of their birth, so that in and of itself is not so remarkable. But Isaiah goes on—the name of this child will be Wonderful, Counselor, Mighty God, Everlasting Father, Prince of Peace.

I wonder whether Isaiah really had any idea what he was writing when he put down those words. Never before had any human being been called Mighty God, Everlasting Father, Prince of Peace. Then he elaborated: "Of the increase of His government and peace there will be no end, upon the throne of David and over His kingdom, to order it and establish it with judgment and justice from that time forward, even forever. The zeal of the LORD of hosts will perform this" (v. 7).

What was Isaiah saying? The heir of David, the son of David, would have an everlasting kingdom—established in judgment and justice, forever!

The kingdom of God was the principal subject of Jesus' teaching. Most of His parables began, "The kingdom of God is like. . . ." When Jesus stood before Pilate, He said, "My kingdom is not of this world" (John 18:36). It's not a limited kingdom, though many have not understood that. Jesus, in the forty days between His resurrection and ascension, taught concerning the kingdom of God. (See Acts 1.)

The son of David who would reign would be no ordinary son. He would be of old, called THE LORD OUR RIGHTEOUSNESS, Wonderful, Counselor, Mighty God, Everlasting Father, Prince of Peace, whose kingdom would be eternal. All of this was prophesied centuries before His birth, so that when He arrived, His people would know He had come.

But did they?

Matthew 12 tells of the Sabbath Day on which Jesus healed a man.

Then the Pharisees went out and plotted against Him, how they might destroy Him. But when Jesus knew it, He withdrew from there. And great multitudes followed Him, and He healed them all.

Yet He warned them not to make Him known, that it might be fulfilled which was spoken by Isaiah the prophet, saying: "Behold! My Servant whom I have chosen, My Beloved in whom My soul is well pleased! I will put My Spirit upon Him, and He will declare justice to the Gentiles. He will not quarrel nor cry out, nor will anyone hear His voice in the streets. A bruised reed He will not break, and smoking flax He will not quench, till He sends forth justice to victory; and in His name Gentiles will trust." Then one was brought to Him who was demon-possessed, blind and mute; and He healed him, so that the blind and mute man both spoke and saw. And all the multitudes were amazed and said, "Could this be the Son of David?" (Matt. 12:14–23).

When Jesus asked the Pharisees, "What do you think of the Christ? Whose Son is He?" and they answered, "The Son of David," they were correct. But they did not know how to respond when He tried to stretch their understanding of what the Son of David was to be. David referred to him as Lord—why? Yet there were the prophecies—pored over by the teachers for hundreds of years.

Son of David, Son of God

Another familiar passage tells of the annunciation of the angel Gabriel to a virgin named Mary.

"Do not be afraid, Mary, for you have found favor with God. And behold, you will conceive in your womb and bring forth a Son, and shall call His name JESUS. He will be great, and will be called the Son of the Highest; and the Lord God will give Him the throne of His father David. And He will reign over the house of Jacob forever, and of His kingdom there will be no end" (Luke 1:30–33).

The angel is announcing that this was to be the fulfillment of those ancient prophecies. Mary's Son was to be also the Son of the Highest, as well as Son of David, with an everlasting kingdom.

"Then Mary said to the angel, 'How can this be, since I do not know a man?' And the angel answered and said to her, 'The Holy Spirit will come upon you, and the power of the Highest will overshadow you; therefore, also, that Holy One who is to be born will be called the Son of God'" (vv. 34–35).

The doctrine of the virgin birth is based on the fact that Jesus was born without the help of a human father. It is found in only this one place in the New Testament. It is not a major teaching of the New

Testament in terms of the amount of space that is given to it. Mark's gospel starts with Jesus at age thirty. John's gospel begins at the start of time, and speaks of Jesus as the Word who was with God, was God, and who became incarnate, but it doesn't go into details about Jesus' birth. Matthew mentions the birth of Jesus only as a fulfillment of the Isaiah prophecy: "The virgin shall conceive and bear a Son, and shall call His name Immanuel" (Isa. 7:14).

However, the doctrine of the virgin birth is crucial to our faith. The incarnation of the Son of God was accomplished by a creative act of the Holy Spirit in the body of Mary, a virgin. It was a special miracle performed by the third person of the Holy Trinity—the Holy Spirit—which enabled the second person of the Trinity—the eternal Son of God—to take upon Himself a genuine, although sinless, human nature. He was born of a virgin, as a man, without surrendering any aspect of His deity. The Holy Spirit of God would not choose to bring forth the Son of God from a human mother who was tainted by sexual sin.

Jesus was the son of Mary, and therefore a human being. He was born into the world just as we were born into it. He went through the various stages of infancy and childhood and all the growth those stages involved. He learned the same way that we do, little by little. He was not God dressed up as a human being. He *was* really human, in all respects like us, except that He remained without sin. It's hard to imagine a human child without sin, and even harder to imagine a human teenager or young adult who was sinless!

Jesus is the Son of God in a unique sense. He is the "only begotten Son of God"—which means He is the only One the Father created through the action of the Holy Spirit. You and I are children of God by faith in Jesus, but we are adopted into the family. Jesus is, as the Nicene Creed puts it, Very God of Very God; but also very man of very man. This may be difficult to understand, but we can understand the concept even if we can't grasp it in our minds. Jesus was fully human and fully divine. He was not just a prophet, He was God. He accepted the worship of people; no prophet ever did that. He was not just a teacher pointing out people's sins. He forgave them; no teacher ever did that.

The question of the Incarnation is a mystery that is answered by each of us. Is it Truth? Jesus asks us, as He asked the Pharisees, "What do You think of the Christ? Whose Son is He?" He was the Son of man, but also the Son of God. The virgin birth was the method by which God brought Jesus into the world. It was God's decision to do it that way—Jesus was His Son! How would you better explain the uniqueness of Jesus? One with us, yet one with God. He had to become man because man was the one who had sinned. He had to be God because God was the only One who could do anything about the sin of man. Humanity had tried for centuries, and the situation only got worse! The only way God could bring about the salvation of the fallen human race was to assume the form of the race He was to redeem.

God has given us the means to know the truth. Jesus is the way to the Father, because He is our Redeemer. He is the truth because He is the fulfillment of all the prophecies concerning Him. He is the life because He overcame death. Think of the Ascension. Jesus returned to the Father not as Spirit, but as resurrected flesh. I think all we will ever see of God when we get to heaven will be Jesus, who has assumed flesh, that we might see Him face-to-face one day. Jesus has the fullness of God dwelling in Him bodily forever and ever. The Son of God became the Son of man so that the sons of men might become the sons of God.

The question is, What is true for you? What do *you* think of Christ? Whose Son is He?

PRAYER

O God, whose glory it is always to have mercy: Be gracious to all who have gone astray from your ways, and bring them again with penitent hearts and steadfast faith to embrace and hold fast the unchangeable truth of your Word, Jesus Christ your Son; who with you and the Holy Spirit lives and reigns, one God, for ever and ever. Amen. —Collect for the Second Sunday in Lent

— QUESTIONS —

What do you think about Jesus?

Is He the One prophesied and promised?

If so, what difference will that make in your life?

How would it make a difference in your world?

CHAPTER 12

Thirsting for Majesty

AN INTERESTING PHENOMENON has occurred in the United States in the past decade or so. We have become royalists! You'd probably never get anyone to admit it, but we have a collective passion for royalty, especially the British House of Windsor.

Millions of people got up in the middle of the night to watch the weddings of Prince Charles to Princess Diana and Prince Andrew to Sarah Ferguson. Magazines constantly print stories about the royal families of Britain, engaging in endless speculation about the status of their health, their marriages, and their offspring. Dolls and books and all sorts of things their fans collect have developed into a small industry surrounding their Royal Highnesses. All this attention in the country that, little more than two hundred years ago, rejected the reign of a British king over them!

This attention is not surprising. Before the British princes were married to such attractive women, the focus was on Princess Grace and Prince Ranier of Monaco. Before them, Arabian Prince Aly Khan and his marriage to movie star Rita Hayworth caught our attention and imagination, and before them the fairy-tale story of the abdication of Edward, Prince of Wales, to marry Wallace Simpson, an American divorcée. I suspect if we were to go back far enough we would find that we have always been captured by the tales of princes and princesses. Certainly generations of children were lulled to sleep with tales of Snow White and Prince Charming, Cinderella, and the like.

The fascination with these stories endures because there is a desire in all of us that I would like to call a thirst for majesty. We thirst for the sense of something larger than our lives, something grander, more noble. Throughout the ages we have been captivated by tales of King Arthur and his Round Table, the stories of the High King of Tara in Ireland, the Czars of Russia, and fabled dynasties of the East. Kings, real and imagined, have ruled well or poorly, and people throughout the ages have sought to have someone to look to whose life would give more meaning to their own—someone whose example they can follow and to whom they can be devoted.

The King of Kings

There is no earthly king who will satisfy us on all counts, but there is a King who will satisfy us completely. He Himself is sought by royalty in the second chapter of Matthew. This passage is the familiar account of the coming of the wise men.

> Now after Jesus was born in Bethlehem of Judea in the days of Herod the king, behold, wise men from the East came to Jerusalem, saying, "Where is He who has been born King of the Jews? For we have seen His star in the East and have come to worship Him." When Herod the king heard this, he was troubled, and all Jerusalem with him. And when he had gathered all the chief priests and scribes of the people together, he inquired of them where the Christ was to be born. So they said to him, "In Bethlehem of Judea, for thus it is written by the prophet:
> 'But you, Bethlehem, in the land of Judah,
>   Are not the least among the rulers of Judah;
>   For out of you shall come a Ruler
>   Who will shepherd My people Israel.' "
> Then Herod, when he had secretly called the wise men, determined from them what time the star appeared. And he sent them to Bethlehem and said, "Go and search carefully for the young Child, and when you have found Him, bring back word to me, that I may come and worship Him also." When they heard the king, they departed; and behold, the star which they had seen in the East went before them, till it came and stood over where the young Child was. When they saw the star, they rejoiced with exceedingly great joy. And when they had come into the house, they saw the young Child with Mary His mother, and fell down and worshiped Him. And when they had opened their treasures, they presented gifts to Him: gold, frankincense, and myrrh. Then, being divinely warned in a dream that they should not return to Herod, they departed for their own country another way (Matt. 2:1–12).

"Where is He who has been born King of the Jews?" was the question posed by the Magi, the kings of the East, or the wise men coming from the East who inquired of Herod where the King of the Jews was to be born. I suppose few stories connected to the birth of Christ have more mysterious aspects to them than the story of the coming of the Magi. This story has been embroidered and enlarged upon considerably down through the centuries by artists and through writers' imaginations, so many aspects of the story as we have become familiar with it really have no basis in Scripture.

We cannot say much with absolute certainty about the wise men from the East. There is no indication in the biblical account that there were three of them. We have traditionally assumed that there were three because of the three gifts mentioned: gold, for a king; frankincense, for the worship of God; and myrrh, for mortal man—a perfume used in embalming. Nowhere do the Gospels say that there were only three—that is tradition.

The Gospels do not indicate that they were kings; yet at least one of the carols familiar at Epiphany heralds the arrival of three kings from the Orient. That tradition is based upon a prophecy found in Isaiah 60, but we have no other evidence that they were kings. They appear to have been religious leaders of a caste from the southern part of Arabia, and were very likely astrologers as well. They had no doubt about what the new star in the sky meant—the birth of the promised King in Judah.

They come to Jerusalem with a strange question, "Where is He who has been born King of the Jews?" They had a clear understanding that there was someone coming who was to be King. The way in which they became aware of these prophecies was through the dispersion of the Jews. In the year 586, when Judea, the southern kingdom of Israel, finally fell to the Babylonians, many people of the land were taken as slaves and scattered throughout the Babylonian Empire. They carried with them their Scriptures and oral traditions, both of which spoke of their expectations of a coming Messiah. We do know from extrabiblical sources that there was a general expectation at the time of Jesus' birth that a great person was to be born, who would emerge as king.

The Magi did not ask, "Has a King of the Jews been born?" They were convinced that he had been born and they came to Herod to inquire as to the place of his birth.

Herod said, in effect, "I have no idea." He summoned the chief priests and the scribes and they said, "According to the prophet Micah, this Coming One is going to be born in Bethlehem."

Born in Bethlehem

There were two Bethlehems: there was Bethlehem Ephrathah in Judea, which is the one referred to here, and there was another Bethlehem, up in the Land of Zebulun, which is in Galilee. How did they know which Bethlehem it was? The answer is in Joshua 19.

Joshua was Moses' successor, and he was the one who led the children of Israel into the land of Promise. After he got them into the land he divided the land among the twelve tribes, and each tribe had its own inheritance in the land. In the book of Joshua, he tells how the land was divided among the tribes. Verse 10 of chapter 19 says the third lot came out for the children of Zebulun and then goes on to list the cities of Zebulun. In verse 15 you will find the city of Bethlehem. This is not Bethlehem of Judea, Bethlehem Ephrathah, but Bethlehem in Zebulun, or Bethlehem of Galilee as it was known in Jesus' day.

In 1 Samuel 17, there is a reference to David: "Now David was the son of that Ephrathite of Bethlehem Judah" (v. 12). Micah the prophet specified that the coming King was going to be born in Bethlehem of Judea or Bethlehem Ephrathah.

The word *Bethlehem* is a compound of words, meaning "house of bread." How significant it is that the one who said, "I am the bread of life which has come down from heaven" should be born in Bethlehem, 'house of bread."

The Magi were aware of the prophecies of the coming King, but they didn't know where He had been born. Scripture says that a star appeared in the sky. There is no way to know whether or not this was a natural phenomenon.

If you go to the Christmas show at the Hayden Planetarium in New York, you will see how they describe the appearance of the star of Bethlehem. With the equipment and records that they have, they are able to reproduce the sky as it appeared at any time in history. They set the time back to 4 B.C. and as you watch, three stars come into line with one another and combine to produce a light of awesome brilliance, which is far greater than anything else in the sky. It appears as though there is only one star, but actually it is a confluence of three that moved together and apparently stayed that way for three years. If the Magi were astrologers and tended to look to the stars and attach significance to them, it may have been that the appearance of this "star" was a signal to them that a long-awaited king had been born.

They might also have gotten the idea from a passage recorded in Numbers 24, one of the prophecies of Balaam. The whole of his prophecy is remarkable, but in the midst of it is this statement: "I see Him, but not now; I behold Him, but not near; a Star shall come out of Jacob; a Scepter shall rise out of Israel" (v. 17). Balaam makes this prophecy to a pagan king: "I look down the corridors of time and see the day when a Star shall rise out of Jacob and a Scepter out of Israel."

We could also simply say that the Lord God, in some mysterious way, revealed to the Magi that they had seen a star that was a sign. So they started out for the land of Israel in order to find this king.

"Where is He who has been born King of the Jews?" they asked when they arrived in Israel. "For we have seen His star in the East and have come to worship Him."

Awaited and Unwanted

We might think that Israel, with a centuries-long expectation of a coming Messiah, would have greeted this news with great joy. But Scripture says Herod was greatly troubled. Herod, by this time, had been king for at least thirty-five years (in all, he was king for thirty-seven years), and he might have thought to himself, "I am king and I have been king for many years. I was made king by Caesar, who gave me this position as a reward to my father who supported him in his campaigns." We can appreciate why he had a problem in welcoming the news that another king had been born.

But Scripture also says that all Jerusalem was troubled with him. Why? Herod certainly was not loved by the people; he didn't do much to inspire love from them. In fact, Josephus, a writer from this period, says it would have been better to have been one of his pigs than one of his sons. Herod was a very hateful man—he was insecure, paranoid, and consumed by jealousy. He put two of his wives to death, and had a number of his children executed at various times. There is a story told that when Herod was close to dying, he knew that there would be great rejoicing in the land at his death. He ordered that eighty of the leading elders of Israel be brought to Jerusalem. They were not told why they were to come; they were just summoned by the king when he was on his deathbed. When they arrived at Herod's palace, they were assembled in a large building where they were locked up until he died.

He had given the order that at his death, the eighty elders of Israel were to be slain, saying, "I am determined to have mourning in Israel at my death." He knew there would not be mourning for him. That order, fortunately, was never carried out.

Herod was more than curious about this new King—he was consumed by the idea.

"And when he had gathered all the chief priests and scribes of the people together, he inquired of them where the Christ (the Messiah, the Anointed One) was to be born. So they said to him, 'In Bethlehem of Judea, for thus it is written by the prophet: "But you, Bethlehem, in the land of Judah, are not the least among the rulers of Judah; for out of you shall come a Ruler who will shepherd My people Israel."'"

It's interesting to compare this quotation of Micah with the actual passage. It appears, as is so often the case, that the quotation was done from memory. People in those days didn't carry Bibles around with them; the Scriptures were large scrolls and they were not generally available. The Scriptures were only familiar to people because they had heard them repeated over and over again. Of course, the religious leaders had studied the Scriptures and had a more precise knowledge, but we will often find that the quotations of the Old Testament found in the New are different, most likely because they were quoted from memory. They are also often quotations of a Greek translation rather than having been taken directly from the Hebrew in which the Old Testament was written. The quotes, then, are loosely given, just as many people today give a loose rendering of a verse that they know is somewhere in the Bible.

Actually, there is an exact reversal of meaning here. Herod's advisors quoted, "You, Bethlehem, in the land of Judah, are not the least among the rulers of Judah; for out of you shall come a Ruler who will shepherd My people Israel." What Micah said was, "Bethlehem, you *are* the least among all the tribes, yet out of you shall come forth a Ruler." This means that the dignity of Bethlehem was not in terms of its great population or its size, but in terms of the mighty and holy One who would come into the world in that place.

"Then Herod, when he had secretly called the wise men, determined from them what time the star appeared. And he sent them to Bethlehem and said, "Go and search carefully for the young Child, and when you have found Him, bring back word to me, that I may come and worship Him also" (vv. 7–8).

That was the height of hypocrisy. Herod took the birth of a king as a threat to his rule. Before he died, Herod had stated in his will that the kingdom be divided among his sons. Archelaus was to rule in Jerusalem, and his other two sons were to have other portions of the country. We can be sure he did not welcome the threatened appearance of another king.

> When they heard the king they departed; and behold, the star which they had seen in the East went before them, till it came and stood over where the young Child was. When they saw the star, they rejoiced with exceedingly great joy. And when they had come into the house, they saw the young Child with Mary His mother, and fell down and worshiped Him" (vv. 9–11).

The next scene after this one relates Herod's order to slay all the male children in Bethlehem under two years of age. We can imagine that a considerable period of time had gone by since the birth of Jesus. I don't want to spoil your Nativity creches with three wise men sweetly placed bearing their gifts to the baby in the manger, but in all likelihood it was not that way at all. The shepherds were there close to His birth, but the wise men almost certainly were not. We don't know when the star appeared, or how long it took the wise men to get to Bethlehem. Scripture does say that they came into a house, not a stable; they found a young Child, not an infant; and Herod gave a decree that all under two years of age should be slain. Why two years? Herod asked the wise men when the star had appeared, so perhaps they related their estimate of about eighteen months to two years ago. Herod very likely wanted a safety margin, and so determined that all the male children under two should be slain. This was not an act calculated to win favor with the people of Bethlehem, so he probably would not have set the age that high if he didn't feel there was a reason to do so.

"And when they had opened their treasures, they presented gifts to Him: gold, frankincense, and myrrh." These were gifts of significance to the wise men and to the culture from which they came. Gold was the prerogative of royalty and speaks of kingship. Frankincense, an incense used in worship, speaks of Jesus as the Son of God, worthy of worship. Myrrh was a precious ointment used in the embalming process; that speaks of His death on the cross. We can see mystic significance in the gifts of the Magi. They were also of value and

significance to the people who brought them; when they visited someone of importance, they would come with significant gifts. Just as the
Queen of Sheba, from the same part of the world as the Magi, came
bearing gifts to Solomon, the wise men presented their gifts. This still
happens: when our President visits a head of state, gifts are ex-
changed.

"Then, being divinely warned in a dream that they should not return to Herod, they departed for their own country another way." One
importance of Epiphany is that it is the first manifestation of Christ to
the Gentiles. He had come, as promised, to the Jews as their Messiah.
But all the way through the Old Testament there were many hints that
He would come to redeem not only the Jews, but all people.

When Jesus was barely a month old He was brought into the temple, where His family encountered a man by the name of Simeon.
Simeon had been told by the Lord that he would not die until he saw
the Messiah, the Lord's Anointed One. When Jesus was brought into
the temple, it says of Simeon: "He took Him up in his arms and
blessed God and said: 'Lord, now You are letting Your servant depart
in peace, according to Your word; for my eyes have seen Your salvation which You have prepared before the face of all peoples, a light to
bring revelation to the Gentiles, and the glory of Your people Israel' "
(Luke 2:28–32).

One theme of the Epiphany season is glory and light. The Scripture
tells us that Jesus was the Son of God and possessed all the glory and
light of the Godhead. Talk about majesty! When He came into this
world, He emptied himself of this glory and came in humility among
us. It was a kind of self-emptying of all the prerogatives of His deity.
He walked among us in obscurity and humility.

There was one moment when three of His disciples—Peter, James,
and John—saw him transfigured on a mountain. It was as though for a
brief moment they saw the glory and majesty of the Son of God just as
He had been from all eternity. In the first chapter of John's gospel we
find these words in verse 14: "And the Word became flesh and dwelt
among us, and we beheld His glory, the glory as of the only begotten
of the Father, full of grace and truth." John says, "I saw the glory of
the Son of God, I'm telling you about it; I'm an eyewitness to His
majesty."

Peter was also there on the Mount of Transfiguration. He makes the
same point:

For we did not follow cunningly devised fables when we made known to you the power and coming of our Lord Jesus Christ, but were eyewitnesses of His majesty. For He received from God the Father honor and glory when such a voice came to Him from the Excellent Glory: "This is My beloved Son, in whom I am well pleased." And we heard this voice which came from heaven when we were with Him on the holy mountain (2 Pet. 1:16–18).

Peter, James, and John saw the majesty of the transfigured Christ; they saw Him as He was from all eternity.

"Jesus spoke these words, lifted up His eyes to heaven, and said: 'Father, the hour has come. Glorify Your Son, that Your Son also may glorify You' " (John 17:1). Jesus prays to the Father to glorify him. "I have glorified You on the earth. I have finished the work which You have given Me to do. And now, O Father, glorify Me together with Yourself, with the glory which I had with You before the world was" (17:4).

Jesus said, "I glorified You on earth having accomplished the work You gave me to do." There is no other way to glorify God! The only way we can glorify God is by accomplishing the work He has for us to do. So often we want to glorify God on our own terms. But the only way we can glorify God is by allowing Him to make us into the people He wants us to be, by doing the things He wants us to do, by being obedient to His word, and by being willing to allow Him to accomplish His purpose in us—that purpose for which we were created. Then when life is done we can say, as Saint Paul did, "I accomplished the task you gave me to do." In so doing we glorify God.

Jesus said, "I have finished; it's all over." "I have finished the work which You have given Me to do. And now, O Father, glorify Me together with Yourself, with the glory which I had with You before the world was" (17:4–5). "And the glory which You gave Me, I have given them, that they may be one just as We are one" (v. 22).

Something resembling the unity of the Godhead Himself is to distinguish the people of God. "Father, I desire that they also whom You gave Me may be with Me where I am, that they may behold My glory which You have given Me; for You loved Me before the foundation of the world" (v. 24).

Somehow, that majestic glory that belongs to the Son of God, which He gave up when He came and walked among us for that brief period of time, that Peter and James and John were allowed for one brief moment to witness, that glory to which He was restored at the Ascension when He returned to the right hand of the Father, that very same majesty and glory He wishes to share with us! That is part of the Christian hope, that one day we shall participate in the majesty of God. And in the meantime, as Paul says in the first chapter of Ephesians, we have been destined to live to the praise of His glory.

Think about the coming of the wise men, Gentiles from a distant place, bringing the best that they had to offer as gifts to the Lord. Think of them going back, no doubt, to spend the rest of their lives saying, as Simeon did, "We have seen the Lord's anointed." Scripture says they returned another way—perhaps this experience changed them somewhat, so that they were different. Consider the majesty of God that appeared in some way to them, and later to the disciples.

The thirst for majesty will never be satisfied by a human king, a human ruler. It is the majesty and the rule of the Son of God that will satisfy us, day-to-day and for all eternity.

PRAYER

Almighty and everlasting God, whose will it is to restore all things in your well-beloved Son, the King of kings and Lord of lords: Mercifully grant that the peoples of the earth, divided and enslaved by sin, may be freed and brought together under his most gracious rule; who lives and reigns with you and the Holy Spirit, one God, now and for ever. Amen.   —Proper 29

— QUESTIONS —

What gifts do you have to offer the King?

How might a living encounter with Jesus affect you?

The wise men sought assistance in finding Jesus. Who might you seek assistance or direction from in order to find Him?

Might a changed direction be in order?

CHAPTER 13

Thirsting for Wisdom

ONE OF THE MOST INTERESTING BOOKS published recently is one titled "An Incomplete Education." Ten years in the making, it is a compendium of information in areas we may never have studied in school but in which society somehow expects us to be well versed. It's done with a bit of humor and a lot of summarizing. Its assumption is interesting: that people needed to know all sorts of things they never learned. I got the impression that the purpose of the book was to help one make a good impression.

This book and others like it point to a basic human desire—a thirst for wisdom. People want to exhibit wisdom, even if superficially. What is wisdom, really? Is it the compounding of facts, figures, and theories in order to be able to hold up your end of a dinner table conversation on any topic? If that's not wisdom, what is? How do we get it?

A relevant question is asked about Jesus in John 7. It was the Feast of Tabernacles, one of the three pilgrimage festivals of the Jewish year, times when the Jews went to the temple at Jerusalem. The feast occurred in the autumn—after the harvest—and lasted for seven days, during which the people dwelt in booths made of the boughs of trees.

Jesus had gone up to Jerusalem for the feast. In the middle of the week He taught in the temple. The people who heard Jesus teaching in the temple were amazed at His wisdom. They asked, "How does this Man know letters, having never studied?" (John 7:15). "Where did He get the degree of understanding He possesses?" They knew He hadn't studied under a famous teacher, such as Gamaliel, yet there was a power in His teaching that left an impression. Where did it come from?

The Source: The Father

Jesus' answer must have puzzled them. "My doctrine is not Mine, but His who sent Me. If anyone wills to do His will, he shall know concerning the doctrine, whether it is from God or whether I speak on My own authority" (vv. 16–17). Right away, Jesus shifted the attention from Himself to His Father, the source of His authority. He said, in essence, "If you're willing to do God's will, then you'll know if what I say is from God. If not, you won't. It's as simple as that."

Although all authority in heaven and on earth belongs to Jesus, when He walked the earth and dwelt among us, He walked as the perfect servant. He was completely submitted to the authority of the Father in all things. Again and again He said, "I did not come to do My own will." "I have not come to speak My own word." The people must have been puzzled at such statements, but they should not have been. Had they been paying attention to the teaching they had received from the Law and the Prophets, they might not have missed the connection.

In the book of Deuteronomy, we find the words uttered by God to Moses in about 1500 B.C.: "I will raise up for them a Prophet like you from among their brethren, and will put My words in His mouth, and He shall speak to them all that I command Him. And it shall be that whoever will not hear My words, which He speaks in My name, I will require it of him" (Deut. 18:18–19).

Willingness and unwillingness to obey was the standard for understanding God's will. It still is.

Isaiah describes the nature of the Branch that would come from the roots of the house of Jesse. "The Spirit of the LORD shall rest upon Him, the Spirit of wisdom and understanding, the Spirit of counsel and might, the Spirit of knowledge and of the fear of the LORD" (Isa. 11:2).

The term *fear* of the LORD also translates "respect" or "obedience." Notice that the Spirit is capitalized. This specifies that when the Spirit of God would come upon the anointed servant, the wisdom, understanding, counsel, might, knowledge, and obedience would come. There would be a specific incident after which the Anointed One would be thoroughly prepared for His appointed task. When was that for Jesus?

Jesus in the Jordan

Jesus was thirty years old when he came to the edge of the Jordan River and submitted to water baptism by His second cousin, John. When He came up out of the water, the heavens opened and a voice was heard to say, "This is My beloved Son, in whom I am well pleased" (Matt. 3:17). That was the moment when Jesus entered into the ministry for which He had come into the world, when He began to function as God's anointed servant and to speak His word. He did not minister until after this event. At that moment the Spirit of wisdom rested upon Him.

The apostle Peter later explained Jesus' baptism in the Jordan to a Gentile by the name of Cornelius:

> The word which God sent to the children of Israel, preaching peace through Jesus Christ—He is Lord of all—that word you know, which was proclaimed throughout all Judea, and began from Galilee after the baptism which John preached: how God anointed Jesus of Nazareth with the Holy Spirit and with power, who went about doing good and healing all who were oppressed by the devil, for God was with Him (Acts 10:36–38).

Jesus Himself testified that His understanding was enlightened by the Holy Spirit, that the source of the authority and power that lay behind His teaching was from none other than God Himself. He didn't claim that the knowledge or the power originated in Him. He claimed only to be the conduit through whom God delivered understanding to those who would "have ears to hear." He was perfectly obedient, so He was an unclogged pipe, so to speak, through which the wisdom of God could flow. Is it any wonder that one of the terms Scripture uses to refer to Jesus is the Word of God?

I've often heard people say that it really isn't so remarkable that Jesus would display such wisdom if He was in fact the Son of God. Those who say that are thinking of Jesus as very God of very God, forgetting that He was also very man of very man. Jesus was conceived by the Holy Spirit, the third person of the Holy Trinity. There never was a moment when He was anything but full of the Spirit of God, but this anointing He received at His baptism was clearly the source of His ministry. He had been full of the Spirit always; now the Spirit was released to pour through Him. He was the first person baptized in the Holy Spirit,

Jesus wasn't just God dressed up like a human being; He was human. When He became human, He gave up all His divine prerogatives. He exercised none of them; He completely laid them aside. As a human being, He learned in the same way that you and I do. He did this for a reason—to show us that there is nothing He did while on earth that we cannot do as well. What He did was the result of the power of the Holy Spirit being manifested through Him.

The gifts He had were gifts that are also available to us, starting with the baptism in the Holy Spirit.

Nazarene Child

The gifts that Jesus exercised—those gifts from the Father through the ministry of the Holy Spirit—were not immediately recognized. One record tells of His visiting His home town, Nazareth. Nazareth was, and still is, an insignificant little town. It has never been a major center of commerce or culture. It is up in the hills of Galilee, and its only importance even today is that Jesus grew up there. No wonder Nathaniel, when he first heard that Jesus was a Nazarene, remarked, "Can anything good come out of Nazareth?"(John 1:46).

Jesus had lived in that little village for thirty years. There was nothing auspicious about His childhood. There wasn't one person in the village who didn't know Him well. When He began to exercise His ministry down by the Sea of Galilee, rumors began to filter back to Nazareth of the marvelous things He was saying and doing.

One day, He decided to take His disciples back to His home town.

> And when the Sabbath had come, He began to teach in the synagogue. And many hearing Him were astonished, saying, 'Where did this Man get these things? And what wisdom is this which is given to Him, that such mighty works are performed by His hands! Is this not the carpenter, the Son of Mary, and brother of James, Joses, Judas, and Simon? And are not His sisters here with us?" So they were offended at Him (Mark 6:2–3).

His old neighbors took offense at the authority with which Jesus taught. Why? Because they had observed Him as a child, a teenager, and a young man, and saw nothing remarkable about Him. They knew Him and His whole family, and they were extraordinarily ordinary.

In my parish there are families whose children I have been privileged to watch grow into adulthood. There were some who were obviously marked for excellence, who seemed to stand out even as small children. That isn't the way it was with Jesus. The townspeople of Nazareth had no high expectations of Him. Even His sinlessness apparently did not draw their notice. Consequently, when reports of His teachings and miracles came back to Nazareth, the townspeople were skeptical. Then, when they heard Him for themselves, they were amazed. Where in the world did He get those ideas?

That's just the point. The source of His wisdom was not of this world. That's why Jesus kept making the point over and over, "My teaching isn't Mine; it's the Father speaking through Me." That is why Moses was told by God that Jesus' words would judge the world, and Isaiah said that people would be judged in terms of how they responded to Jesus' words, because they were God's words. People still will be judged on the same basis.

The anointing of the Holy Spirit upon Jesus gave Him the power to do what He did for God. It wasn't because He was the only begotten Son of the Father—He had relinquished all "perks" that went with that. He took upon Himself our nature, with all its limitations. He learned about God, and God's will for Him, in the same way that we do—gradually.

His knowledge grew, and when He was twelve years old, His parents took Him up to the temple to become a "son of the commandment"—what we know today as "bar mitzvah," a full member of the religious community. But in questioning Him, the teachers were amazed. ". . . they found Him in the temple, sitting in the midst of the teachers, both listening to them and asking them questions. And all who heard Him were astonished at His understanding and answers" (Luke 2:46*b*–47).

That early understanding came about because He pored through the Scriptures, He inquired, and He came to an understanding that nobody else in His generation shared. He saw that it was God's will that the Messiah die for His people. That wasn't a result of the revelation to the Messiah-to-be; it wasn't through some sort of special communication. He learned it through study. He learned through prayer, just as we do. The only difference is that His mind was never crowded with sinful thoughts as ours are. He was tempted, but it didn't take root in His mind or heart. But the Scriptures, the written words of God, did.

The Spirit-Filled Person

Jesus was, and is, the perfect example of a Spirit-filled person. The Spirit of God rested upon Him, and all the manifestations of the Spirit were produced in His life.

Let's look at what 1 Corinthians 12 says about the so-called "gifts of the Spirit." It begins by saying "But the manifestation of the Spirit is given to each one for the profit of all" (v. 7).

Well, that certainly applies—Jesus said He came to serve the whole world. What this means for us is that any manifestation of the Spirit that God may choose to exercise through us—any that we allow to flow from Him—are not for our glory, but God's. We can never lay claim to having a particular ministry that is based on a gift the Holy Spirit makes available through us. It is His, not ours. It is to be used to bless those God chooses to bless. This requires submission and availability.

"For to one is given the word of wisdom through the Spirit, to another the word of knowledge through the same Spirit" (v. 8). Many times people marvelled at the wisdom and knowledge of Jesus. Here Paul says these were gifts of the Spirit, manifestations of the work of the Holy Spirit that flowed without interruption through Jesus. It was said of Jesus that He had no need for any man to tell Him about man, because He knew what was in them. That knowledge, that discernment, came as a result of the work of the Holy Spirit. So it can be with us. We may thirst for wisdom and seek knowledge, but unless we seek the Holy Spirit first, we will experience only a poor counterfeit.

"To another faith by the same Spirit" (v. 9a). There's no question about it—Jesus possessed faith in abundance and He acted upon it. Many times He found Himself in a tight spot, and if God had not come through, He would have had a problem. But He spoke the word of the Spirit confidently and Lazarus came forth from the tomb. He spoke to the seas and they were still. He spoke to deaf ears and they heard. The faith He had was from the anointing of the Holy Spirit resting upon Him. Do you have faith? It is the result of the work of the Holy Spirit in your life.

"To another gifts of healings by the same Spirit" (v. 9b). There are so many examples of Jesus' healing ministry. Where did His healing power come from? It came from the same anointing that is available to us. He was God's anointed servant from the time of His baptism in the Spirit onward. He was always God's Son, and He must have met countless sick people before He was baptized in the Jordan, yet there is no record of His having healed one person prior to that experience.

I want to take a stand against the teaching that says that if we have enough faith, we will be healed. There is absolutely no evidence in Scripture to sustain that. They are separate gifts, separate manifesta-

tions of the work of the Holy Spirit in and through the followers of
Jesus Christ. A person needing the gift of healing does not need to be
manifesting faith in exceptional quantities. The gift of faith need not
be present at all. God sovereignly chooses how, when, and who He
heals. Sometimes He chooses to heal them ultimately, by calling them
to Himself. Faith cannot determine the results, but can help us accept
God's answers—"yes," "in time," or "not the way you expect."

"To another the working of miracles" (v. 10). What miracles? The
multiplication of the loaves and fishes, the walking on water, and so
many others. His ability to perform those miracles came not because
He was the Son of God, but because it was the will of the Father that
those things be manifested through Him. And He said that we would
do greater things than these!

"To another prophecy" (v. 10). Remember the Deuteronomy passage? Jesus was spoken of as a prophet. A prophet is a spokesman for
God, someone who speaks His words. Jesus said, "I do not speak My
own word, but the word of the Father and these words are to you as
life and health and strength" (see John 6:63; 14:24). We should beware when we hear a "prophecy" given in church that makes us
afraid or sounds harsh and judgmental. If the words of prophecy don't
bring life and health and strength, they are not of the Lord God.

"To another discerning of spirits" (v. 10). This is commonly called
"discernment." When Peter made his great confession "You are the
Christ, the Son of the Living God" (Matt. 16:16), Jesus said, "You're
right, Peter, but flesh and blood did not reveal that to you, but My
Father who is in heaven." Peter's understanding didn't come from
study or experience. It was a revelation of the Father to Peter.

But when Jesus started to tell the disciples of the purpose for which
He came into the world, and said that He must go to Jerusalem and
die, Peter's response was from the flesh. "Far be it from You, Lord."
And Jesus' response was "Get behind Me, Satan." Jesus had dis-
cerned, in Peter's words, the voice of God one moment and the voice
of Satan the next. What happened with Peter can happen to us—we
have clogged channels. Our will at times is against God's will. If
someone manifests the gift of discernment, he or she will be able to
help us sort out the voices, the motivation we are following.

"To another different kinds of tongues, to another the interpretation
of tongues" (v. 10). The gift of tongues is largely misunderstood.
"Tongues" is a private prayer language given by the Spirit to aid the
communication, heart-to-heart, of the Christian with God. Have you

ever felt so helpless in a situation that you didn't know how to pray? Have you ever been so caught up in the worship of God that you ran out of things to say? The gift of tongues is manifested for these purposes.

People who allow this gift to flow freely in their lives sometimes have multiple tongues—different cadences, sounds, and rhythms. For example, a praying mother might be given one tongue that she hears herself use when she prays for her children, and another for her husband. Some pray aloud in worship services, and some sing in tongues. These gifts used in public require some sort of interpretation, which is yet another manifestation. Interpretation must always be measured against Scripture to know it is valid. The Holy Spirit will never speak against the witness of the Word of God, written or Person.

The Helper

What is the action of the Holy Spirit that enables these gifts to function? Let's look at a few verses from the Gospel of John. These are words of Jesus, explaining things to his disciples. "Nevertheless I tell you the truth. It is to your advantage that I go away; for if I do not go away, the Helper will not come to you; but if I depart, I will send Him to you" (John 16:7).

The Spirit is here called "the Helper"—in some translations, "the Counselor"—as one called alongside to help. We often refer to a lawyer as "counselor," and we expect a lawyer to help, not hinder, our case. What is the Helper's function? To be present with us and to whisper in our spiritual ears those things that are necessary for our life in Christ.

"Most assuredly, I say to you, he who believes in Me, the works that I do he will do also; and greater works than these he will do, because I go to My Father" (14:12). Because Jesus went to be with the Father, we will do the same things that He did and greater, with the aid of the Holy Spirit.

"And I will pray the Father, and He will give you another Helper, that He may abide with you forever—the Spirit of truth, whom the world cannot receive, because it neither sees Him nor knows Him; but you know Him, for He dwells with you and will be in you" (vv. 16–17). The Spirit of truth has been given to us. Hadn't Jesus said He was the way, the Truth, and the Life? The world could not receive Jesus. Here Jesus is telling us that the Holy Spirit is His Spirit; He will send us the Spirit of truth, His own Spirit, to reside in us.

"But the Helper, the Holy Spirit, whom the Father will send in My name, He will teach you all things, and bring to your remembrance all things that I said to you" (v. 26). It is the Holy Spirit, the gift of Christ, who will teach us. We will have the same source of wisdom that Jesus Himself had.

"But when the Helper comes, whom I shall send to you from the Father, the Spirit of truth who proceeds from the Father, He will testify of Me" (15:26). Another manifestation of the Spirit of God is to be able to testify to Jesus. You can only confess Christ as Lord by the power of the Holy Spirit working through your life.

> However, when He, the Spirit of truth, has come, He will guide you into all truth; for He will not speak on His own authority, but whatever He hears He will speak; and He will tell you things to come. He will glorify Me, for He will take of what is Mine and declare it to you. All things that the Father has are Mine. Therefore I said that He will take of Mine and declare it to you" (16:13–15).

The Holy Spirit's guidance will never be different from that of the Father and the Son. Are you sensing what you believe to be a leading of the Spirit? Check it out in Scripture. If you can't find validation there, validation doesn't exist.

Are you beginning to get the picture? The source of Jesus' miraculous power to heal, to do miracles, to discern, to speak with power and wisdom, all these came to Him because He was a yielded vessel through whom the Holy Spirit could flow freely. And Jesus says that the same Holy Spirit will come to us, and lead us into an understanding of the truth of God. He will lead us to Jesus; He will empower us; He will equip us for greater works than even Jesus did.

Christian Anointing

If the word *Christ* means "Anointed One," then what does the word *Christian* mean? "Anointed Ones." The very same anointing that equipped Jesus for His life of ministry and service is not only available to us, but is sort of a basic requirement for Christian service.

The apostle John wrote to those who were struggling against false teachings: "But you have an anointing from the Holy One, and you know all things. . . . But the anointing which you have received from Him abides in you, and you do not need that anyone teach you; but as the same anointing teaches you concerning all things, and is true, and is not a lie, and just as it has taught you, you will abide in Him" (1 John 2:20, 27).

If the anointing of the Spirit is basic equipment, wouldn't you think we need to learn to use it? It starts with trust. We have to trust that the gift has been given in response to prayer. We have to trust in Jesus' promise.

We must also be yielded. Yielding is an act of the will. The degree to which the Holy Spirit will flow through us is the degree to which we are yielded, obedient, seeking, and open.

Think of the flow of water through a hose. We are like hoses—to be used to give the life-giving water of God to the world. The power is released into us as water is released into the hose, and should flow freely from it. But with a hose, if someone bends it or ties it in a knot or steps on it, it will slow the flow to a trickle, or ultimately stop it.

Can you be bent? Can you be persuaded that the things of God are not true? Can you be tied in knots? Can the circumstances of life twist your perspective and pull you so tight that nothing gets through? Can you be stepped on? Will people's opinions of you and judgment upon your ministry matter so much to you that the Spirit is stopped?

The world thirsts for the wisdom of God to counteract the lies of His enemies. Will you be a part of the means by which He waters His world?

PRAYER

O God, whose blessed Son made himself known to his disciples in the breaking of the bread: Open the eyes of our faith, that we may behold him in all his redeeming work; who lives and reigns with you, in the unity of the Holy Spirit, one God, now and for ever. Amen.
—Collect for the Third Sunday of Easter

— QUESTIONS —

Which of the gifts of the Spirit do you currently find manifested in your life?

Which of the gifts of the Spirit do you desire?

What blocks the channel through which the Holy Spirit must flow through you to others?

How could you use the help of the Helper right now?

CHAPTER 14

Thirsting for Victory

NOT LONG AGO, I was at an airport when the local baseball team arrived home from winning a significant series of games. There were hundreds of people waiting for them—avid fans with horns, confetti, signs, and champagne. It was quite a scene. I wondered at the devotion that was inspired by a seemingly innocuous game. (My son, Everett Jr., would strongly disagree with me. He prefers the Mets; I prefer the Met.) Perhaps I should not have been surprised at the strength of the devotion of the team's fans. In sports or any other endeavor of life, everybody loves a winner. We want to share in the thrill of victory; it is a constant thirst.

It is precisely that thirst for victory that makes us squirm a bit at the events of Holy Week. From the world's point of view, Christians haven't been cheering the winner. From God's point of view, nothing could be further from the truth. The story of Gethsemane and Golgotha is the story of the greatest victory that was ever won.

The story starts with a victory Jesus won while He walked the earth.

Now a certain man was sick, Lazarus of Bethany, the town of Mary and her sister Martha. It was that Mary who anointed the Lord with fragrant oils and wiped His feet with her hair, whose brother Lazarus was sick. Therefore the sisters sent to Him saying, "Lord, behold, he whom You love is sick." When Jesus heard that, He said, "This sickness is not unto death, but for the glory of God, that the Son of God may be glorified through it." Now Jesus loved Martha and her sister and Lazarus (John 11:1–5).

Jesus did not leave immediately, He stayed where He was for two more days. Then He said it was time to go to Judea. The disciples were concerned about this, and reminded Jesus that it was dangerous for Him to return to Judea, since the leaders had tried to stone Him there. Jesus answered: "Are there not twelve hours in the day? If anyone walks in the day, he does not stumble, because he sees the light of this world. But if one walks in the night, he stumbles, because the light is not in him" (vv. 9–10). Jesus' answer to the disciples was that He could safely go back into dangerous territory as long as He was walking in the light of His Father's will.

These things He said, and after that He said to them, "Our friend Lazarus sleeps, but I go that I may wake him up." Then His disciples said, "Lord, if he sleeps he will get well." However, Jesus spoke of his death, but they thought that He was speaking about taking rest in sleep. Then Jesus said to them plainly, "Lazarus is dead. And I am glad for your sakes that I was not there, that you may believe. Nevertheless, let us go to him" (vv. 11–15).

Jesus knew Lazarus had died before He went to Bethany. He knew it was the will of the Father for him to be raised up, and that the disciples needed to witness it. Others needed to learn from this event, too.

Scripture says that Lazarus had been dead four days by the time Jesus arrived at Bethany. Martha came out to meet Him, but Mary stayed in the house in mourning.

Now Martha said to Jesus, "Lord, if You had been here, my brother would not have died. But even now I know that whatever You ask of God, God will give you." Jesus said to her, "Your brother will rise again." Martha said to Him, "I know that he will rise again in the resurrection at the last day." Jesus said to her, "I am the resurrection and the life. He who believes in Me, though he may die, he shall live. And whoever lives and believes in Me shall never die. Do you believe this?" (vv. 21–26).

He was challenging her faith. She responded, "Yes, Lord, I believe that You are the Christ, the Son of God, who is to come into the world" (v. 27).

Martha then went and told Mary that Jesus was on His way. Mary came out of the house, and those who were with her in mourning followed her, thinking she was going to Lazarus's tomb. Mary ran to Jesus and fell at His feet. "Lord, if You had been here, my brother would not have died" (v. 32). Jesus saw her weeping, and all those who were with her weeping, and groaned in His spirit and was troubled. He wept, also. Those who were with them thought He wept because He loved Lazarus. But His next words give an indication that He wept for other reasons, as well.

He went to the tomb and had them roll away the stone in spite of being warned about the stench of a decaying body, saying, "Did I not say to you that if you would believe you would see the glory of God?" It was the lack of faith in those who were so close to Jesus that caused Him pain. He knew the purpose and the victory of God; that is evident in His prayer. "Father, I thank You that You have heard Me. And I know that You always hear Me, but because of the people who are standing by I said this, that they may believe that You sent Me" (vv. 41*b*–42). And then He cried with a loud voice, "Lazarus, come forth!" And the rest, as they say, is history.

The raising of Lazarus from the dead was one of the principal events that hastened the death of Jesus upon the cross. It increased the antagonism of the chief priests and scribes against Him. Raising Lazarus was clear evidence of the power Jesus had over life and death. It was a mighty miracle, and it moved great numbers of people to believe that Jesus was indeed the Messiah.

"Now a great many of the Jews knew that He was there; and they came, not for Jesus' sake only, but that they might also see Lazarus, whom He had raised from the dead. But the chief priests plotted to put Lazarus to death also, because on account of him many of the Jews went away and believed in Jesus" (John 12:9). Again, in verse 18: "For this reason the people also met Him, because they heard that he had done this sign."

It was a tremendous miracle that captivated the imagination of the crowd. News of Lazarus's resurrection brought scores and scores of people to the city of Jerusalem, eager to welcome their Messiah when He came riding into the city.

Disappointed Expectations

Jesus, of course, saw their expectations as He rode into the city. He knew that what they expected was not at all what He had come to do. They proclaimed Him as King, and King He was. But the kind of kingdom over which He ruled was not at all the kind of kingdom they imagined. They were looking for a political Messiah to throw off the Roman domination. Jesus came to throw off the true, eternal enemies of man—sin, death, and the devil—and to establish the rule of God in the hearts of men. He knew that what He planned to do would frustrate their expectations of Him. He said: "The hour has come that the Son of Man should be glorified. Most assuredly, I say to you, unless a grain of wheat falls into the ground and dies, it remains alone; but if it dies, it produces much grain. He who loves his life will lose it, and he who hates his life in this world will keep it for eternal life" (John 12:23–25).

Jesus was not above applying His own teaching to Himself. He was tempted to escape the fate that awaited him, but He determined to fulfill the will of the Father: "Now My soul is troubled, and what shall I say? 'Father, save Me from this hour'? But for this purpose I came to this hour" (v. 27).

It is as though Jesus is thinking out loud, saying, "Shall I pray that God would deliver me?" He knew the fickleness of the crowd. He knew that the same people who were crying "Hosanna to the Son of David. Blessed is He who comes in the name of the Lord!" would in a few days be crying "Crucify Him!" He knew that, although He rode into the city on the crest of a wave of popularity, when the people discovered that He was not going to fulfill their expectations, that the kingdom He had come to establish was not of this world, they would turn against Him. The same crowd that was singing praises to Him as He entered the city would be calling for His death in a very short period of time.

Jesus clearly understood that fulfilling the role of Messiah involved His death. To the common people of Israel, the Messiah was not one who had come to be rejected and die. They thought of the Messiah as One coming with all the might and power of David and the glory of Solomon, to restore Israel to a prominence it had not had for nearly a thousand years. They thought only in terms of the physical restoration of the kingdom of Israel, in the world's terms. They had no real understanding of the nature, function, role, and ministry of God's Messiah, His promised Servant. Jesus, in studying the Scriptures, came to understand a deeper view of this One whom God was calling into the world.

He understood the prophetic words of Isaiah. The Jewish people generally did not understand the prophet Isaiah. This might be why they missed God's plan. Through Isaiah, the Lord said: "I am going to establish the kingdom; I am going to set up a king, who shall be a child who is going to be born to you. He will be called Everlasting Father, Almighty God, Prince of Peace." That passage ends by saying "The zeal of the LORD of Hosts will perform this" (Isa. 9:7). There is never any question in Isaiah's writings that God is going to carry out His purpose!

In Isaiah 53, the prophet writes in the past tense even though it will be nearly seven hundred years before this word is fulfilled. He writes in the past tense as though the event had already been accomplished, so certain was he that God would bring about His plan. He begins, "Who has believed our report? And to whom has the arm of the LORD been revealed?" (v. 1). Who can understand what this means? To whom has the arm of the Lord—God's hand, God's purpose—been revealed? Then he turns immediately to the center of the purpose of God and says, "For He shall grow up before Him as a tender plant, and as a root out of dry ground. He has no form or comeliness; and when we see Him, there is no beauty that we should desire Him" (v. 2).

Jesus of Nazareth certainly came from a very unpropitious place, for what good thing ever came out of Nazareth? David's line had now been cut off for over five hundred years. Surely it was dry ground. Who would expect that out of these unpromising circumstances a shoot would begin to come forth? Not only that, but Isaiah says clearly that He had no form or comeliness, no beauty that we should desire Him. By prophetic insight, the word is laid down that this Coming One was not going to be physically appealing or attractive. Nothing about Him in terms of His physical characteristics would have attracted anyone, by human estimation.

"He is despised and rejected by men, a Man of sorrows and acquainted with grief. And we hid, as it were, our faces from Him; He was despised, and we did not esteem Him" (v. 3). Isaiah writes prophetically of the Coming One and says, "Nobody holds Him in esteem. He was rejected; He was acquainted with sorrow; He was despised by the people, so much so that they would not even look at Him." This tells us what God was doing. "Surely He has borne our griefs and carried our sorrows; yet we esteemed Him stricken, smitten by God, and afflicted" (v. 4). This Messiah was to be no winner in the eyes of the world.

Some years ago I was flying into Israel from Istanbul and my seat companion was a young Jewish boy about eighteen or nineteen years old, who lived in the Bronx. It was his first trip to Israel. He was very anxious to see the land of his fathers, as he was a very Orthodox Jew. I noticed during our trip that at certain times of the day, he took out his phylacteries—small leather boxes containing the law of Moses—and strapped them to his wrists and forehead for his time of prayer.

We talked a lot on that flight. When we got to Jerusalem I told him of an inexpensive hotel where he could stay, and took him there. I knew that since we arrived late Friday afternoon, just before the beginning of the Sabbath, the first thing he would want to see would be the Wailing Wall. I offered to take him to it. As we wandered down the narrow streets of the Old City of Jerusalem I could see the effect it was having on him; he was very somber and subdued. Finally we came out into the area near the temple mount. I knew he would not enter the temple area, because no Orthodox Jew will go there lest he step on the spot where the Holy of Holies once was. Since no one knows exactly where it was, no Orthodox Jew will go on the temple mount; they will keep to the area of the Wailing Wall.

We walked on until the Wailing Wall was in front of us. On Friday evening, it is crowded with all sorts of people who come there to pray facing the wall, and it is well lit. Tradition says that the Wailing Wall is the one place where all prayers go straight to God, so people go right up to the wall to say their prayers. They often leave little notes with prayer requests in the crevices between the blocks of stone. We stood there and watched this moving spectacle for a long time.

When we were ready to move on, I finally asked him, "What do you think of Jesus Christ?" He said, "Well, I know that you Christians think it was we Jews who put Him to death, crucified Him. But," he said, "you know what I believe? I believe that God put Him to death because of His blasphemy. He got exactly what He deserved because He claimed to be God. I think it was a judgment upon Him." I responded, "This is amazing. Here we are, standing close to the spot where it all happened, and you are saying to me something that one of your prophets almost three thousand years ago said that you would say." We went back to this remarkable passage in Isaiah 53, verse 4: "Surely He has borne our griefs and carried our sorrows; yet we esteemed him stricken, smitten by God, and afflicted."

That's what my young friend thought had happened, that God had smitten Jesus for blasphemy. But Isaiah goes on to say, ". . . He was wounded for our transgressions. He was bruised for our iniquities; . . . All we like sheep have gone astray; we have turned, every one, to his own way; and the LORD has laid on Him the iniquity of us all" (vv. 5*a*, 6). So I went on to explain to him that I didn't believe the Jews had killed Jesus, nor did any Christians who knew Scripture well. I told him that Scripture makes it clear Jesus had come into the world for this purpose—to die—and that it was God's plan for victory, not defeat.

Jesus had seen these same Isaiah passages, and had thought about them. He clearly saw that God's servant was going to be sent into the world to die for God's people.

> He was oppressed and He was afflicted,
> Yet He opened not His mouth;
> He was led as a lamb to the slaughter,
> And as a sheep before its shearers is silent,
> So He opened not His mouth.
> He was taken from prison and from judgment,
> And who will declare His generation?
> For He was cut off from the land of the living;
> For the transgressions of My people He was
>   stricken" (vv. 7–8).

Who understood? No one but Jesus. The disciples didn't know what was going on. They thought that when Jesus was crucified, this was a fair indication that He couldn't have been the Messiah! They didn't understand that He was indeed being stricken by God, and that He was being wounded for our transgressions, smitten for the sins of God's people.

"And they made His grave with the wicked—but with the rich at His death, because He had done no violence, nor was any deceit in His mouth" (v. 9). Jesus was crucified between two thieves, and was buried in the borrowed tomb of a rich man, Joseph of Arimathea.

The next verse makes the point that was so difficult for my young Jewish friend, and many others throughout the ages, to understand. "Yet it pleased the LORD to bruise Him; He has put Him to grief. When You make His soul an offering for sin, He shall see His seed, He shall prolong His days, and the pleasure of the LORD shall prosper in His hand. He shall see the labor of His soul, and be satisfied" (vv. 10–11a).

Jesus' death was the will of the Lord. My young friend was partially right—it really was the Lord who put him there, but not in judgment. Jesus said, "No man takes my life from Me, but I lay it down

Myself." Jesus' crucifixion was an act of willing self-sacrifice. Why? So that we could make His sinless soul an offering for our sins. This is how His kingdom comes—we are His seed, His harvest. The Father's pleasure is in receiving those who trust in what Isaiah calls the labor of Jesus' soul—His crucifixion—as satisfaction for their sins.

Jesus has always had a hard time getting that message across.

Who Do Men Say That I Am?

Let's look at the first occasion when Jesus told the disciples what was going to happen to Him. Jesus did not tell them until He had some indication that they understood who He was. Jesus came into the area of Caesarea Phillipi, and gathered His disciples and said, "Who do men say that I, the Son of Man, am?" (Matt. 16:13). And they replied, "Some say John the Baptist, some Elijah, and others Jeremiah or one of the prophets" (v. 14). Jesus wasn't satisfied with that answer, so He pushed them a little further: "But who do you say that I am?" (v. 15). I imagine there might have been an awkward pause, then Peter spoke out and said, "You are the Christ, the Son of the living God" (v. 16).

Jesus replied, "Peter, you are absolutely right. But flesh and blood hasn't revealed this to you, but My Father in heaven." All that Peter had observed, and all that they had shared, had not convinced Peter that Jesus was the Christ. The Holy Spirit had sort of a breakthrough in Peter at that moment.

After that confession of faith as to who He really was, Jesus began to tell them what needed to happen:

> From that time, Jesus began to show to His disciples that He must go to Jerusalem and suffer many things from the elders and chief priests and scribes, and be killed, and be raised the third day. Then Peter took Him aside and began to rebuke Him, saying, "Far be it from You, Lord; this shall not happen to You!" But He turned and said to Peter, "Get behind Me, Satan! You are an offense to Me, for you are not mindful of the things of God, but the things of men" (Matt. 16:21–23).

The very suggestion that He not go to Jerusalem, that He not die, that He disobey the will of the Father, was regarded as an intrusion of Satan—because this was the reason for which Jesus had come into the world. The disciples were still caught in the mindset of men.

So Jesus tried again, after the Transfiguration. Think about this: Peter, James, and John had just seen Jesus transfigured, in heavenly glory, and had seen Moses and Elijah with Him. What an extraordinary experience! He told the disciples not to tell anyone about the vision until after He was risen from the dead. Wouldn't you think it would have made an impression?

"Now while they were staying in Galilee, Jesus said to them, 'The Son of Man is about to be betrayed into the hands of men, and they will kill Him, and the third day He will be raised up.' And they were exceedingly sorrowful" (Matt. 17:22–23).

Jesus told His disciples that it was soon going to be necessary for Him to be betrayed and to die. But He also told them that on the third day He would be raised up. Did they rejoice at the victory that would represent? No, they were exceedingly sorrowful. They still did not understand. Jesus had to give it another try:

Now Jesus, going up to Jerusalem, took the twelve disciples aside on the road and said to them, "Behold, we are going up to Jerusalem, and the Son of Man will be betrayed to the chief priests and to the scribes; and they will condemn Him to death, and deliver Him to the Gentiles to mock and to scourge and to crucify. And the third day, He will rise again" (Matt. 20:17–19).

It was perfectly clear to Jesus that it was the will of His Father that He allow Himself to be crucified. He knew He would be betrayed, mocked, scourged, and crucified. He also knew He would rise again. He was trying to get that message across to the people who were closest to Him.

When Jesus was arrested in the Garden of Gethsemane, Peter cut off the ear of the high priest's servant with his sword. Jesus said, "Put away your sword, Peter; don't you know that I could call legions of angels and they would deliver me? And if they did, how then could the Scriptures be fulfilled?" It's not that Jesus couldn't have avoided the cross; He chose not to do so. He willingly died in obedience to the Father, that the Scriptures might be fulfilled, so that those who would come to faith would know and understand what He had done.

Saint Paul describes this tremendous self-sacrifice of Jesus. "Who, being in the form of God, did not consider it robbery to be equal with God, but made Himself of no reputation, taking the form of a bond-servant, and coming in the likeness of men. And being found in appearance as a man, He humbled Himself and became obedient to the point of death, even the death of the cross" (Phil. 2:6–8).

We will miss the significance of the crucifixion if we think Jesus was a young man who came to a tragic end—a martyr who tried to teach something that couldn't be accepted by this world, and who died an untimely death. That is not the case at all. Jesus saw Himself as fulfilling the eternal purpose of God. Peter, in speaking of this on the Day of Pentecost, said that according to the foreknowledge of God, Jesus went to the cross. In His life as a servant, He came to obey His Father, and it was the will of His Father that He give His life as a ransom for many.

Hard Choice

Realizing that Jesus knew and accepted that the will of the Father led to His death brings us to examine more closely the whole account of Jesus in the Garden of Gethsemane. When we think of that time, we think of His struggle.

> Then Jesus came with them to a place called Gethsemane, and said to the disciples, "Sit here while I go and pray over there." And He took with Him Peter and the two sons of Zebedee, and He began to be sorrowful and deeply distressed. Then He said to them, "My soul is exceedingly sorrowful, even to death. Stay here and watch with Me." He went a little farther and fell on His face, and prayed, saying, "O My Father, if it is possible, let this cup pass from Me; nevertheless, not as I will, but as You will" (Matt. 26:36–39).

Many people have interpreted this passage as though Jesus, in the weakness of His human flesh, is asking to be delivered from His impending death. It seems to me that interpretation is not in line with the witness of the rest of Jesus' words. Such a prayer seems totally out of harmony with everything we know about Him. He had said clearly to His disciples, over and over again, "I have come to die." He rebuked Peter when he even made a suggestion that He should not die. Are we to imagine, then, in this last moment of agony in the garden, that Jesus cried out "Father, I don't want to do it! But if You will, I will go through with it"? What is the "cup" He is asking to have removed? I think the cup from which Jesus recoils is the cup of the wrath of God against evil.

In Isaiah 51 the prophet speaks about drinking the cup of trembling, the dregs of the cup of the fury of God's wrath. John 16 speaks of the bowls, or cups, of the wrath of God poured out because of sin. I think Jesus was recoiling from the thought that all the evil in the world was about to be placed upon Him. He, who knew perfect fellowship and harmony with His Father, was about to be separated from Him because of the sins of the world. That is the only way to explain His cry on the cross: "My God, My God, why have You forsaken Me?" Why? Because in that hour He became sin for us, that we might become the righteousness of God in Him. He tasted the full power of God against evil and against sin; and in order to do so, He had to drink of the cup of His Father's wrath.

Jesus always prayed in harmony with the will of God, so we have to ask ourselves, was this prayer answered? If it meant avoiding the crucifixion, then of course His prayer was not answered. He didn't avoid death; He actually went through with it. But look at what precedes His prayer in the garden.

"Then Jesus came with them to a place called Gethsemane, and said to the disciples, 'Sit here while I go and pray over there'" (Matt. 26:36). He took Peter, James, and John with Him, and told them: "My soul is exceedingly sorrowful, even to death. Stay here and watch with Me" (v. 38).

Then He went a bit farther away from them and prayed. He came out later and found His friends asleep. "The spirit indeed is willing, but the flesh is weak," He said. "Watch and pray, lest you enter into temptation" (v. 41). I think here He was also speaking of Himself.

The Gethsemane account describes Jesus sweating great drops of blood, a kind of perspiration that is indeed blood. Medical professionals have found that in times of great physical and mental agony such a thing can happen to people. Something happens and blood begins to come out of their pores almost as if it were perspiration. When that happens, death is quick to follow. "My soul is sorrowful even unto death," Jesus said. It seems to me that Jesus was afraid Satan would gain victory over Him if He died in the garden. Jesus had come to die on a cross and so, in His prayer, He is asking to be strengthened.

In Hebrews we find a most unusual passage, and we might ask as we read it, What incident in the life of Jesus does this refer to? ". . .in the days of His flesh, when He had offered up prayers and supplications, with vehement cries and tears to Him who was able to save Him from death, and was heard because of His godly fear, though He was a Son, yet He learned obedience by the things which He suffered" (Heb. 5:7–8).

The only time that we know of this happening is the incident in the Garden of Gethsemane. The prayer was answered; angels came and ministered unto Him and strengthened Him so that He would be obedient, and God would have the victory.

Where Is the Victory?

Is there a lesson in this incident for us? Have we glimpsed the means of attaining the victory that Jesus won? Actually, He won a series of victories—a victory over the influences of the world, a victory over the weakness of the flesh, and a victory over the devil. Jesus won them through obedience to God's purpose and through prayer. Not just a little prayer in passing, but a prayer that caused Him to sweat His life's blood. He was strengthened to be able to fulfill the purpose of God. There was so much at stake!

Jesus understood clearly that this was why He came, and He rebuked those who even suggested otherwise. He lived, as we do, in a frail body—a body that had limitations on the amount of suffering that it can handle, a body that can yield to death even when the spirit is strong. He won that bitter contest in Gethsemane. The Father sent His angels to surround Him and to strengthen Him. Will He do less for us in our struggles?

The problem is, in order to expect the help of the Father to attain our own victory, we must be sure that we are being obedient to the plan and the purpose of God. If we expect God to bless or help us with something that is not in line with His revealed will, then we will have frustrated expectations, as did the Jewish people who expected the Messiah to come in a political realm. Remember that Jesus said the Scriptures must be fulfilled. This is true today. If our lives are in line with the revelation of Scripture, if our prayers are in line with the revelation of Scripture, then the Holy Spirit is able to work most effectively to bring about God's desired victory in our lives. The world, the flesh, and the devil will have no power over us if we are submitted, obedient, and prayerful. God's victory will be ours!

PRAYER

O God, who for our redemption gave your only-begotten Son to the death of the cross, and by his glorious resurrection delivered us from the power of our enemy: Grant us so to die daily to sin, that we may evermore live with him in the joy of his resurrection; through Jesus Christ your Son our Lord, who lives and reigns with you and the Holy Spirit, one God, now and for ever. Amen.   —Collect for Easter Day

— QUESTIONS —

Do you have frustrated expectations of God?

Are your expectations, hopes, and prayers in line with the revelation of Scripture?

To what things in your life do you say, "The spirit is willing, but the flesh is weak"?

How are you at watching and praying?

CHAPTER 15

Thirsting for Resurrection

THE TRAGIC CRASH of Pan Am flight 103 in Lockerbie, Scotland just before Christmas of 1988 caught the attention of the entire world. The trauma and pain of those who lost loved ones became a part of our lives; their loss was ours. The impact hit especially hard due to the combination of raw violence and so many wonderful young lives ended. Three young people from our area were on that flight, and as the press reported the comments of their friends and families, we had a sense of stolen potential, unrealized dreams, and of how much poorer the world will be because these young people cannot contribute to its future.

In the midst of all that tragedy, the voice of hope was still proclaimed. Could we dare to look beyond the moment—to a life that continued, though it was separate from what we experienced now? The nation was thirsting for resurrection; and try as they could, the media could do little to assuage the thirst.

The Inescapable Question

In the book of Job, a question is asked that has been asked since the very beginning of time: "If a man dies, shall he live again?" (14:14).

No group of people on the face of the earth has not raised that question and tried in some way to answer it. There seems to be a universal yearning for life beyond what we call life. Scripture tells us that God has put eternity into our hearts. There is something offensive to the human spirit at the thought that the grave is really the end of our existence.

Certainly we will all die. What we call death is the common lot of kings and servants, rich and poor, wise and foolish, male and female.

It is not possible to live in this world and not have to ask that question. Basically, there are only three possible answers.

No, Yes, or Immortal?

We will find one answer to this question reflected in the book of Ecclesiastes. In this fascinating book, we look into the heart of a cynic, a person who had everything that the world had to offer and yet found that his heart's desire was not satisfied. This author was a person in desperate straits. The author is said to be Solomon, and these are his thoughts as he was gradually straying from the Lord. And here is his response to the question, "If a man dies, shall he live again?"

> I said in my heart, "Concerning the condition of the sons of men, God tests them, that they may see that they themselves are like animals." For what happens to the sons of men also happens to animals; one thing befalls them: as one dies, so dies the other. Surely, they all have one breath; man has no advantage over animals, for all is vanity. All go to one place: all are from the dust, and all return to dust. Who knows the spirit of the sons of men, which goes upward, and the spirit of the animal, which goes down to the earth? (3:18–21).

Here is the reflection of a man embittered by life, a man who has found all that he had sought after with such vigor has turned to ashes in his hand. Life left a bitter aftertaste in his mouth. He reflects on the inevitable death of men, and says, "Isn't it the same thing for man and beast? Don't they all go from dust to dust? When you lower a body into a grave, that's the last you'll ever see of that person." There are many who believe that, though I suspect not without a tug at the heart at the thought of such senseless loss.

But almost as if to show his dissatisfaction with his conclusion, he raises a question at the end. "Who knows whether the spirit goes down to the earth?" Even in the depths of his despair, he raises the possibility that there might be a difference between man and beast.

Finally, at the end of the book, the writer of Ecclesiastes seems to have come to another mind on the subject. He describes old age and death, and says: 'Remember your Creator before the silver cord is loosed, or the golden bowl is broken, or the pitcher shattered at the fountain, or the wheel broken at the well. Then the dust will return to the earth as it was, and the spirit will return to God who gave it" (12:6–7).

The images speak of loss of life support. Life is fragile; death interrupts it. But, says the writer, if you remember your Creator while you live, then the dust will return to the earth as it was, and the spirit will return to God who gave it. That would be a second answer: "Yes, there is life after death."

Immortality

There is a third position—probably the one best known and most widely held—and that is the view that human beings are somehow created immortal. Not in bodily terms, certainly. Our bodies are very transitory by nature; they grow old and decay even before we die. But many believe that the spirit of human beings is immortal and will never die. That was the conviction of Plato and most of the Greek philosophers, and many Christians and non-Christians believe the same thing. But immortality is not a Christian concept. Nowhere in Scripture are we taught that the soul is by nature immortal!

In Genesis we read how God created humanity out of the dust of the earth. A chemist who broke down our physical bodies into their chemical components would find iron, calcium, phosphorous, and other elements similar to those found in the ground. God fashioned man of the dust of the earth, but He breathed into him the breath of life, and he became a living soul. The question is, "Is that soul, from that moment on, forever alive?" Plato said yes. But the second chapter of Genesis tells the story differently.

> And out of the ground the LORD God made every tree grow that is pleasant to the sight and good for food. The tree of life was also in the midst of the garden, the tree of the knowledge of good and evil. . . . Then the LORD God took the man and put him in the garden of Eden to tend and keep it. And the LORD God commanded the man, saying, "Of every tree of the garden you may freely eat; but of the tree of the knowledge of good and evil you shall not eat, for in the day that you eat of it you shall surely die" (Gen. 2:9, 15–17).

I don't need to retell the whole story. Suffice it to say that Adam and Eve used the precious freedom that they had been given to disobey the Lord. They partook of the forbidden fruit. The Lord put them out of the garden, and put a cherubim at the gate to restrain them from returning to the garden.

"Then the LORD God said, 'Behold, the man has become like one of Us, to know good and evil. And now, lest he put out his hand and take also of the tree of life, and eat, and live forever—'" the statement is not finished, but the next verse says that the Lord God sent Adam out of the garden to till the ground from which he was taken (vv. 22–23).

Man was created by God as potentially capable of gaining immortality. The tree of life was a tree of which he could freely have eaten, by the will of God. After sin entered, the Lord blocked the way to the tree of life, lest, in his rebellious state, he partake of it and live forever. In the garden man forfeited his right to immortality.

The Lord had said, "In the day that you eat of it you shall surely die." Well, Adam and Eve didn't die physically that day, but they did die spiritually. They died in terms of their relationship to God. They went and hid themselves. That is the nature of our separation from God; we try to hide our actions and our thoughts from others and from ourselves. When there is little openness, that is a sign of spiritual death. Spiritual death, when it has taken its full toll, results in physical death. The letter to the Romans tells us that death entered the world through and because of sin. Man has forfeited the possibility of gaining immortality on his own, by the will of God.

God's Immortality

Only God is immortal by nature. Paul tells Timothy:

> I urge you in the sight of God who gives life to all things, and before Christ Jesus who witnessed the good confession before Pontius Pilate, that you keep this commandment without spot, blameless until our Lord Jesus Christ's appearing, which He will manifest in His own time, He who is the blessed and only Potentate, the King of kings and Lord of lords, who alone has immortality, dwelling in unapproachable light, whom no man has seen or can see, to whom be honor and everlasting power. Amen (1 Tim. 6:13–16).

If we are not immortal, then how do we obtain eternal life? Jesus said:

> For as the Father raises the dead and gives life to them, even so the Son gives life to whom He will. For the Father judges no one, but has committed all judgment to the Son, that all should honor the Son just as they honor the Father. He who does not honor the Son does not honor the Father who sent Him. Most assuredly, I say to you, he who hears My word and believes in Him who sent Me has everlasting life, and shall not come into judgment, but has passed from death into life (John 5:21–24).

The New Testament teaching is not that everyone has eternal life, but that those who come to God through Jesus Christ are given eternal life as a gift. Many passages contain this teaching; it is not found in only one or two texts. The new birth, being "born of the Spirit," is to have the life of God given to us. Not all are born of the Spirit. The Scripture rejects the idea that everybody has a spark of deity within. In fact, the Bible says that man, in his natural condition, is "dead to God" and that rebirth, an action of the Holy Spirit, is required to plant the life of God.

That "the gift of God is eternal life" doesn't mean that our lives just go on and on and on. It means that we share in the divine nature of God, which is itself eternal. It is His life, then, that is lived in our bodies. That's what's meant by eternal life. We don't begin eternal life when we die; we begin it while we still live. Eternity begins with belief in Christ.

"And as Moses lifted up the serpent in the wilderness, even so must the Son of Man be lifted up, that whosoever believes in Him should not perish but have eternal life. For God so loved the world that He gave His only begotten Son, that whoever believes in Him should not perish but have everlasting life" (John 3:14–16). Eternal life comes to those who believe in the Son of Man, who has been lifted up on the cross—that act of obedience to the Father, His death, that brought salvation to all who believe in Him. It belongs to those who will share in the resurrection victory of Jesus Christ over death.

"He who believes in the Son has everlasting life; and he who does not believe the Son shall not see life, but the wrath of God abides on him," John the Baptizer said, after he baptized Jesus (v. 36). The witness of the Holy Spirit was clear from the beginning of Jesus' ministry: eternal life is a gift of God to all who believe in Him.

Jesus acknowledged that not everyone would believe in Him, but that eternal life was for those who did.

Now it was the Feast of Dedication in Jerusalem, and it was winter. And Jesus walked in the temple, in Solomon's porch. Then the Jews surrounded Him and said to Him, "How long do You keep us in doubt? If You are the Christ, tell us plainly." Jesus answered them, "I told you, and you do not believe. The works that I do in My Father's name, they bear witness of Me. But you do not believe, because you are not of My sheep, as I said to you. My sheep hear My voice, and I know them, and they follow Me. And I give them eternal life, and they shall never perish; neither shall anyone snatch them out of My hand" (10:22–28).

Eternal life belongs to those who follow Jesus, and nothing can take this gift from them. The promise of Jesus is this: "I am the resurrection and the life. He who believes in Me, though he may die, he shall live. And whoever lives and believes in Me shall never die. Do you believe this?" (11:25–26).

Do You Believe?

This, then, is the Christian hope. There is no universal assurance that all will have eternal life, either to be spent eternally with God or eternally in hell. The word used to describe those who do not find eternal life is that they "perish." There is no indication that they languish eternally in hell. That notion arose precisely because of the Platonic teaching of the immortality of the soul. Obviously, if you have an eternal soul and you're not with God, then you've got to be somewhere; that idea led to the thought that is generally accepted as Christian teaching. But the Bible teaches that those who are not with God perish—they end. There is no eternal life for them.

The Scripture does seem to say, in both the Old and New Testaments, that there will be a resurrection of all the dead. Daniel says that the resurrection includes the righteous and the unrighteous; the New Testament says the same thing, that all will be raised. The purpose of the resurrection is that great moment when God will vindicate Himself before the eyes of the whole world.

There will come a day when every last human being will see and understand perfectly what God has been doing. We are told that in that day, every knee will bow to Jesus Christ, and every tongue will confess that He is Lord. All will bow, but some will find Him not the Lord that they have been waiting for, but the Judge. He will judge the living and the dead. And those who are judged and found wanting, without the salvation of Jesus Christ, will perish. Those who share in the resurrection of Jesus will live for all eternity.

Central Teaching

The resurrection of Jesus is the central point of the faith of the Christian church. If there is no resurrection, there is no Christianity.

Some years ago I took a course in the history of religions at Harvard Graduate School. Some of the world's most distinguished scholars came in and spoke for several weeks on the various religions of the world. When it came time to study Christianity, the lecturer was Dr. Arthur Darby Knock from Oxford University. He had written the *Oxford History of the Christian Church*. He brilliantly traced the preparation through the prophets, explained the act of God in Jesus' ministry and death, and then lectured on the Resurrection. I will never forget his plain statement.

"Gentlemen, if you don't believe in the Resurrection, you have the problem of explaining the history of the Christian church. There never would have been any church if there had not been a Resurrection. Those disciples would never have reconvened after the Crucifixion, had they not seen the risen Lord. That was the motivation that gave the church its power. They were willing to die for it, because they knew that God had vindicated His Son and raised Him from the dead, and they would be raised also. If Christ is not raised, then there is no basis for the Christian faith, and we'd better forget it as fast as we can."

In the last chapter of Luke, you can clearly see the discouragement of the disciples after the Crucifixion.

> Now behold, two of them were traveling that same day to a village called Emmaus, which was seven miles from Jerusalem. And they talked together of all these things which had happened. So it was, while they conversed and reasoned, that Jesus Himself drew near and went with them. But their eyes were restrained, so that they did not know Him. And He said to them, "What kind of conversation is this that you have with one another as you walk and are sad?" Then the one whose name was Cleopas answered and said to Him, "Are You the only stranger in Jerusalem, and have You not known the things which happened there in these days?" And He said to them, "What things?" So they said to Him, "The things concerning Jesus of Nazareth, who was a Prophet mighty in deed and word before God and all the people, and how the chief priests and our rulers delivered Him to be condemned to death, and crucified Him. But we were hoping that it was He who was going to redeem Israel. Indeed, besides all this, today is the third day since these things happened. Yes, and certain women of our company, who arrived at the tomb early, astonished us. When they did not find His body, they came saying that they had also seen a vision of angels who said He was alive. And certain of those who were with us went to the tomb and found it just as the women had said; but Him they did not see" (24:13–24).

These followers of the Lord could not get past the fact that He had died. Luke says that their "eyes were restrained." Even though He had told them what was to be, they could not see beyond the tragedy of His death. They could not see He had risen, even when He walked with them. How much, I wonder, is our sight restrained by the focus we place on what has happened around us? How often do we miss seeing the Lord in the midst of our circumstances?

Jesus answered them, "O foolish ones, and slow of heart to believe in all that the prophets have spoken! Ought not the Christ to have suffered these things and to enter into His glory?" And next Luke says that "beginning at Moses and all the Prophets, He expounded to them in all the Scriptures the things concerning Himself" (vv. 25–27). What a Bible study that must have been!

Cornerstone of Apostolic Teaching

Later on, when He appeared to the eleven disciples, Jesus said that all these events were laid down in the Old Testament. "Then He said to them, 'These are the words which I spoke to you while I was still with you, that all things must be fulfilled which were written in the Law of Moses and the Prophets and the Psalms concerning Me.' And He opened their understanding, that they might comprehend the Scriptures" (Luke 24:44–45).

It was prophesied that the Messiah should die and be raised. In the Nicene Creed, which we recite in our parish every week, we say we believe that "on the third day he rose again in accordance with the Scriptures." The Scriptures the creed refers to are the Old Testament prophecies.

Several passages in the book of Acts show that the witness to Jesus' resurrection from the dead was absolutely central to the teaching of the apostles. After the Crucifixion, Judas went out and hanged himself, which left eleven disciples. Jesus' followers decided that there really should be twelve. They probably saw themselves as being the counterparts for the twelve tribes of Israel. They set down certain qualifications: "Therefore, of these men who have accompanied us all the time that the Lord Jesus went in and out among us, beginning from the baptism of John to that day when He was taken up from us, one of these must become a witness with us of His resurrection" (Acts 1:21–22).

The prime qualification for Judas' replacement was that he had to have been with them through the entire time of Jesus' ministry—from the baptism by John in the Jordan to His Ascension, which had just occurred. Two men who fulfilled those qualifications—Joseph called Barsabbas, and Matthias. "One of these must become a witness with us of His resurrection." They saw their apostolic function not in terms of the length of time that they walked with the Lord, or how much they recalled of His teachings, but largely in that they were witnesses to the fact that Jesus had been raised from the dead.

Further evidence of this idea is given in Peter's sermon on the day of Pentecost.

> Men of Israel, hear these words: Jesus of Nazareth, a Man attested by God to you by miracles, wonders, and signs which God did through Him in your midst, as you yourselves also know—Him, being delivered by the determined purpose and foreknowledge of God, you have taken by lawless hands, have crucified, and put to death: whom God raised up, having lossed the pains of death, because it was not possible that He should be held by it. For David says concerning Him: "I foresaw the LORD always before my face, for He is at my right hand, that I may not be shaken; therefore my heart rejoiced, and my tongue was glad; moreover my flesh also will rest in hope, for you will not leave my soul in Hades, nor will you allow Your Holy One to see corruption. You have made known to me the ways of life; You will make me full of joy in Your presence" (Acts 2:22–28).

Peter asserts that Jesus was the one of whom David spoke, that He had risen from the dead, and that eternal life was possible through Him. "This Jesus God has raised up, of which we are all witnesses. Therefore being exalted to the right hand of God, and having received from the Father the promise of the Holy Spirit, He poured out this which you now see and hear" (v. 34).

The cornerstone of apostolic teaching was the resurrection of the dead. Acts 4 says that as they spoke to the people the leaders were greatly disturbed that they taught the people and preached in Jesus the resurrection from the dead.

Peter wasn't the only one to give voice to the resurrection's centrality to the faith. The apostle Paul preached in Antioch:

> Now when they had fulfilled all that was written concerning Him, they took Him down from the tree and laid Him in a tomb. But God raised Him from the dead. He was seen for many days by those who came up with Him from Galilee to Jerusalem, who are His witnesses to the people. And we declare to you glad tidings—that promise which was made to the fathers. God has fulfilled this for us their children, in that He has raised up Jesus (Acts 13:29–33*a*).

Paul wrote to the church at Corinth that the Resurrection was of prime importance: "For I delivered to you first of all that which I also received: that Christ died for our sins according to the Scriptures, and that He was buried, and that He rose again the third day according to the Scriptures" (1 Cor. 15:3–4).

Here's why it is so important: "And if Christ is not risen, your faith is futile; you are still in your sins! Then also those who have fallen asleep in Christ have perished. If in this life only we have hope in Christ, we are of all men the most pitiable" (vv. 17–19). If Christ has not risen, we are to be pitied because we have no other way of dealing with our sins.

Jesus' Resurrection and Ours

The gospel message is that Jesus was raised from the dead! There is a connection between Jesus' resurrection and ours. Jesus said, "Because I live, you shall live also." The assurance of that resurrection is ours by faith.

There is an obvious question in relation to this assurance, one which occurs to people as they begin to consider the resurrection of the dead. "But someone will say, 'How are the dead raised up? And with what body do they come?' " (1 Cor. 15:35).

That which dies is perishable. The body decays; it returns to the earth. Death is an indignity whenever it occurs, whatever the circumstances. Death is an enemy. Death is an insult to life. There is something impertinent about the ending of a life that was intended to live to the praise of God's glory forever. The good news is that death has been defeated! The Bible does not try to soften death at all, but rather faces it and recognizes that it is not the end for those who are in Christ Jesus.

How are the dead raised up? And with what kind of body? Paul answers, "It is sown a natural body, it is raised a spiritual body. There is a natural body, and there is a spiritual body" (v. 44).

The natural body that we inhabit will never see heaven. It is a physical body, and it will return to the dust from which it was created. The spiritual body is given by God. We will be given new and glorified bodies. "Behold, I tell you a mystery: We shall not all sleep, but we shall all be changed—in a moment, in the twinkling of an eye, at the last trumpet. For the trumpet will sound, and the dead will be raised incorruptible, and we shall be changed" (vv. 51–52).

That day will come when we are clothed with our heavenly bodies, when we have immortality. Putting it on means that we don't have it. It is not part of our natural disposition.

I recall a question that was asked of me by a woman whose husband had died. "Where is he now? What do we believe? Is he with Jesus now or is he waiting for the last day?" I answered, "Don't you see, it doesn't make any difference." Heaven and eternity are outside of time as we know it. We can't even conceive of what that means. Basically, by the time our loved ones realize they have been clothed in their heavenly bodies and turn to show them to others, we will be with them. "To be absent from the body is to be present with the Lord," Paul said. We are caught in time waiting to be reunited with them, but they have no time to miss us as we miss them.

Paul contrasts our present body with the body that will one day be ours: "For we know that if our earthly house, this tent, is destroyed, we have a building from God, a house not made with hands, eternal in the heavens. . . . Now He who has prepared us for this very thing is God, who has also given us the Spirit as a guarantee" (2 Cor. 5:1, 5).

The Bible knows nothing of a heaven where spirits float about. The idea of a human spirit without a body is referred to as nakedness. It is incomplete. Our spiritual beings have bodies, and they are eternal. The disease, sickness, weariness, and all those things that are part of our earthly experience are not present in our heavenly bodies. They cannot decay. They are perfect reflections of our spiritual selves, and they are ours for eternity due to our faith in the resurrection of Jesus Christ.

> He who believes in the Son of God has the witness in himself; he who does not believe God has made Him a liar, because he has not believed the testimony that God has given of His Son. And this is the testimony: that God has given us eternal life, and this life is in His Son. He who has the Son has life; he who does not have the Son of God does not have life" (1 John 5:10–12).

Did you know it is possible to call God a liar? If a person does not believe that Jesus is the Son of God, who came to earth to die for our sins and rose again in victory, that person calls God a liar, and the eternal life of God is not possible for them. This truth goes against the popular theme of universal salvation and eternal life for all. God has determined His way to eternity, and whether or not we believe it is up to us.

Access to the Tree of Life

In the last chapters of the Bible, the book of Revelation, there is a description of the heavenly city. John describes the New Jerusalem as being square, about fifteen hundred miles on each side. He saw a wall that was about 216 feet tall, made of jasper. The city itself seemed to be made of pure gold. It had streets and buildings, but they were like clear glass. The foundations of the city were adorned with all kinds of precious stones in all colors of the rainbow. The twelve gates were made of twelve pearls; each gate was a pearl, and the gates were always open. John saw no temple in it, "for the Lord God Almighty and the Lamb are its temple" (21:22). There was no need for a temple. The sacrifice was done; the people were in the presence of God.

There was no need of the sun or the moon, either, John said, because the glory of God gave the city light. There was a pure river of the water of life, proceeding from the throne of God and of the Lamb.

And in the middle of heaven, John saw an interesting thing. "In the middle of its street, and on either side of the river, was the tree of life, which bore twelve fruits, each tree yielding its fruit every month. The leaves of the tree were for the healing of the nations" (22:2).

There's the tree from which we were banished in the garden. It is now in the heavenly city. And John heard these words: "Blessed are those who do His commandments, that they may have the right to the tree of life, and may enter through the gates into the city" (v. 14).

The tree of life, which in Genesis could enable man to live forever, is the right of all those who do God's will, who believe in His Son, and who know His resurrection. Thanks be to God who gives us resurrection to life eternal!

PRAYER

Almighty God, who through your only-begotten Son Jesus Christ overcame death and opened to us the gate of everlasting life: Grant that we, who celebrate with joy the day of the Lord's resurrection, may be raised from the death of sin by your life-giving Spirit; through Jesus Christ our Lord, who lives and reigns with you and the Holy Spirit, one God, now and for ever. Amen.

—Collect for Easter Day, 3

— QUESTIONS —

Jesus said His sheep hear His voice, and follow Him. Do you?

If your heavenly body perfectly reflects your spirit, what will yours be like?

Is the fact of the resurrection of Jesus Christ a comfort to you? Or does it upset you because of lack of faith?

CHAPTER 16

Thirsting for Commitment

ONE OF THE MOST IMPORTANT BOOKS of the decade, if not the century, is Charles Colson's "Kingdoms in Conflict." In it he explains in very readable terms the basic struggle between church and state, the kingdom of God and the kingdom of men. He points out the decline of the influence of the Judeo-Christian tradition in the world and the corollary decline in the moral and ethical climate of society. Without credence or commitment being given to absolute standards, the laws are meaningless. If there is no good or evil, if everything is relative, on what can we base our choices? We thirst for commitment to absolutes.

A story in 1 Kings makes the point of the necessity of choosing God and committing to His ways. It is the story of the conflict between the worship of Baal and the worship of God. Baal worship was introduced to Israel during the reign of King Ahab, by his wife Jezebel. Jezebel had been a Sidonian princess before she married the king of Israel, and when she came to live in Israel, she brought with her 450 priests and prophets of her ancestral religion.

Baal worship was a pagan worship. It was conducted inside temples or, in good weather, outside on high hilltops. Worship included animal sacrifice, ritualistic meals, and licentious dances. There were temple prostitutes of both sexes; human fertility symbols were part of their altars. The word *baal* itself meant master, and Baal was supposedly the son of El, the father of all of the gods and the head of the Canaanite pantheon of gods. He is also known as the son of Dagon, a deity associated with agriculture. Baal was thus the god who supposedly gave increase to family and field, flocks and herds.

The introduction of pagan worship into Israel was devastating. People were drawn to the loud, flashy services and lured into thinking that they could cover their bases by worshiping both God and Baal. Finally, the prophet Elijah came upon the scene. He challenged the people of Israel to make up their minds. The question he asks them is very clear: "How long will you falter between two opinions? If the LORD is God, follow Him; but if Baal, follow him" (1 Kings 18:21).

There comes a time when a person has to make up his or her mind as to what god to serve. The god that ultimately concerns you is the one that will command your best efforts, your time, your talents, your resources. Your choice of gods will determine who you are and how you act toward the world around you. If you are a citizen of a particular realm, you will take on the appearance of the inhabitants of that realm, or kingdom.

If we have chosen to allow Jesus to be Lord, then we are in His kingdom. This means that, as Paul said, "He has delivered us from the power of darkness and conveyed us into the kingdom of the Son of His Love, in whom we have redemption through His blood, the forgiveness of sins" (Col. 1:13–14). Jesus said that we must realize we cannot serve two masters—we will hate the one and love the other.

Kingdom of Darkness

The Scriptures speak of a kingdom of darkness whose sovereign's name is Satan. His name means "adversary." Satan has been described as "the god of this world," who blinds people's minds to the truth of Jesus Christ. He is a master at deception and counterfeit, he is adept at persuasion, and he specializes in indulgence of the flesh. He is also called "the prince of the power of the air" who opposes the rule of Christ and controls evil movements and unjust political systems.

He has working under him a hierarchy of demonic powers, described as "principalities and powers," whose job is to persecute, accuse, and infiltrate the world. The New Testament mentions the existence of the spirits of error, lust, and fear, as well as unclean spirits, seducing spirits, deaf and dumb spirits, lying spirits, familiar spirits (as in the occult), and many others.

Recently I have encountered a strain of teaching that gives a lot of credit to the power of Satan. The good news of the gospel delivers people from the fears of Satan's power over them. It's very important to understand what Scripture says about Satan.

First, he exists. One of the greatest lies abounding in the church today is that there is no such thing as the devil. Satan's greatest job of deception is convincing believers that he does not exist! But since the days of the early church, there has been a continuous line of serious teaching about the unseen battle for the souls of men between Satan and God. The existence of Satan is taught in seven Old Testament books and by every New Testament writer. Jesus acknowledged and taught the existence of Satan.

Second, Satan is a vanquished foe, and he knows it! He has lost the battle. The only power that Satan and his forces can exercise over you is the power that he is able to persuade you he has over you. He will use his intellect, his emotions, and his will to influence yours.

Do you recall the account of Jesus' temptation in the wilderness? It is the first thing that happened after His baptism by water and the Spirit.

"Then Jesus was led up by the Spirit into the wilderness to be tempted by the devil" (Matt. 4:1). He was led by the Spirit of God into the wilderness where He was tempted. Satan did not creep up on Him and spring on Him with all kinds of schemes. Jesus saw that the wilderness was a divine appointment for Him. His encounter with Satan did not originate in hell (which also exists), but in the mind and the heart of the Father, who wanted Him to vanquish and defeat Satan and all of his forces. Even at the Crucifixion, where Satan's power was most manifest, Jesus saw clearly that it was the Father who sent Him to the cross, not Satan.

Let's see what, in fact, God has done in reference to Satan.

First, He brought His Son into the world. "For this purpose the Son of God was manifested, that He might destroy the works of the devil" (1 John 3:8). That's why Jesus came—to overcome the one who had brought the earth under his dominion and control.

The conflict started in Eden. The Lord God said that He would put enmity between the serpent and the descendant of the woman. "He shall bruise your head, and you shall bruise His heel" (Gen. 3:15). Clearly, from the beginning of the conflict, Satan knew that his reign was limited.

When Jesus cried out on the cross, "It is finished!" He wasn't saying, "It's all over, I've failed." That wasn't it at all—it was a cry of triumph, a cry of victory! He was shouting for the Father and all the universe to hear, that the purpose for which He came into the world was done. Satan's power had been destroyed.

Notice that I said Satan's power had been destroyed—not Satan. Satan's own destruction is certain, but it comes at the last day. His power has been overcome, however, since Jesus' death on the cross. From that time on Satan's power has been a matter of choice.

"Inasmuch then as the children have partaken of flesh and blood, He Himself likewise shared in the same, that through death He might destroy him who had the power of death, that is, the devil, and release those who through fear of death were all their lifetime subject to bondage" (Heb. 2:14–15).

Jesus became flesh so that through the experience of death of the flesh He might be able to destroy the devil, who had the power of death, and release those who were in bondage. This means that Satan's forces can only have influence in areas where Jesus does not have full reign. Think of it in terms of a battlefield. Your life is the field on which a battle is being fought, inch by inch. One side holds a certain amount of territory; the other holds the rest. Those areas that are not subject to the lordship of Jesus Christ are held by His adversary.

The Kingdom of God

There is also the kingdom of God. When John the Baptizer began to preach, he said, "Repent, for the kingdom of heaven is at hand." Much of Jesus' teaching centered on this important concept of the kingdom of God. He often started His parables by saying, "The kingdom of heaven is like. . . ." During the forty-day period between the resurrection of Jesus and His Ascension and return to the Father, the Scripture tells us that He spoke to His disciples of the kingdom of God.

I am often asked for a one-sentence definition of the kingdom of God. I always refer the inquirers to the Lord's Prayer, in which Jesus told us to pray, "Your kingdom come, Your will be done on earth as it is in heaven" (Matt. 6:10). I believe the kingdom of God is simply a state of affairs where the will of God is perfectly carried out. The kingdom of God is present to the degree that people submit themselves to the sovereignty of Jesus Christ. The question is, what kingdom and what dominion do you serve under as a Christian? Have you, in fact, been taken out of the kingdom of darkness and transferred into the kingdom of light?

If not, then you are not a Christian in any sense of the word. You may be civilized, you may have your name on a church roll, but you cannot consider yourself a Christian. Jesus said that it requires a new birth to be a Christian. It's such a radical thing, that it's like starting life all over again. We must be born again, and learn life all over from a different perspective, if we are to see the kingdom of God. This is what happens when a person comes to the point of being able to profess a faith in Jesus Christ, trusts Him as Savior, and invites Him to be Lord of his or her life. That is how a person is born again and brought into the kingdom of God.

"Seeing the kingdom" has everything to do with the way you understand and interpret your life. I had an experience once that dramatized this point for me. I was on my way to a speaking engagement, being driven there by a friend. We had not left any extra time, and we had a flat tire on the way. What was worse, we didn't have a spare. We realized at exactly the same moment that we were not going to be able to get there on time. We both made declarative statements, absolutely contrasting in nature. He said, "Look how Satan is seeking to hinder us in proclaiming the message tonight!" At that same time, I said, "I wonder what God has in mind by allowing this delay?" Which was it? Should we interpret the things that happen from Satan's point of view, or from God's? Can we see the kingdom of God in the events of our lives?

Temptation

Well, you might say, "I believe in Jesus. It's just that I succumb to temptation sometimes." I'd like to look at the matter of temptation. The word *temptation* means a kind of seduction or persuasion to do something evil. James provides a profound psychological description of temptation: it begins with a desire. "Let no one say when he is tempted, 'I am tempted by God'; for God cannot be tempted by evil, nor does He Himself tempt anyone. But each is tempted when he is drawn away by his own desires and enticed" (James 1:13–14).

I don't know about you, but I've never seen Satan running around dressed in a red suit with horns, tail, and pitchfork. I think we could handle a Satan that came to us that way! But he is much more subtle than that. Satan begins by working within the hearts of people, working in their desires. Temptation is not sin. Jesus was tempted in every way we are, but without sin. It is not sinful to be tempted. Temptation becomes sin when we yield to the desire, when we commit a sinful act. Ultimately, spiritual death is the end product.

How are we to understand the place of temptation in the Christian life? James has the answer to that, too. "My brethren, count it all joy when you fall into various trials, knowing that the testing of your faith produces patience. But let patience have its perfect work, that you may be perfect and complete, lacking nothing" (James 1:2–4).

The NKJV uses the word "trials." The Greek word can be translated either as "trials" or as "temptations." Think of trials as difficulties. These can become temptations; they can lead you to sin. For instance, if you are struggling with a disease, the temptation could arise to say to God, "Why have you allowed this to happen to me?" The temptation arose from the circumstances of the trial.

There is a reason for temptation and for trials. The problems we encounter in our everyday lives, the things that seem insurmountable at times, are intended to be means for our sanctification. Those things that lead us to discouragement are meant to help us grow! Those things that tempt us are designed to increase our steadfastness! If we are untried and untested, then we have no strength. Progressive resistance builds up our spiritual strength just as it does our physical strength. That is the only way we can become the mature Christians God wants us to be.

God's purpose in allowing temptation is to help us endure. Barclay's translation says it so well: "My brothers, you must regard it as nothing but joy when you are involved in all kinds of trials. For you must realize that when faith has passed through the ordeal of testing the result is the ability to pass the breaking point and not to break."

That's the result of a tested life. God doesn't tempt us to evil, but He always allows us to be in situations of testing, continually and forever, because this is the way He produces commitment, endurance, and maturity in us.

How long will you go on limping with two different opinions? If the Lord is God, then follow Him. If Baal, then him. The Baals of this world are of the same source—the world culture, the flesh, the devil. Which interpretation will you hold for your life?

You have to make a choice in almost everything you do. You have to make the commitment to Christ over and over and over again—not in terms of going forward in a worship service and saying the sinner's prayer time and time again, but in choosing to follow God's ways in whatever you do.

Moses makes this point to the people of Israel as they were preparing to enter the Land of Promise:

> See, I have set before you today life and good, death and evil, in that I command you today to love the LORD your God, to walk in His ways, and to keep His commandments, His statutes, and His judgments, that you may live . . . . But if your heart turns away so that you do not hear, and are drawn away, and worship other gods and serve them, I announce to you today that you shall surely perish; . . . I call heaven and earth as witnesses today against you, that I have set before you life and death, blessing and cursing; therefore choose life, that both you and your descendants may live; that you may love the LORD your God, that you may obey His voice, and that you may cling to Him, for He is your life and the length of your days (Deut. 30:15–20*a*).

Understand the limitations of Satan's realm. Imagine a stake driven into the ground, and tethered on a long chain attached to it is a roaring and ravenous lion. A person walks through the door, a tasty morsel to the lion's eyes. The lion takes one look at him and makes a flying leap, but is caught by the chain on his neck. He cannot reach. Now, if that person desires, he or she can walk within the reach of that chain, whereupon the lion would have a feast. That's the way it is: Satan has no power over your life that you do not grant him. He has been bound; his power is limited. But heed the words of Peter: "Be sober, be vigilant; because your adversary the devil walks around like a roaring lion, seeking whom he may devour. Resist him, steadfast in the faith, knowing that the same sufferings are experienced by your brotherhood in the world" (1 Pet. 5:8–9).

In Matthew 12 Jesus speaks of binding the strong man. I hear people pray for others, binding Satan over the problem. That's completely unnecessary! Satan is bound and he knows it! The very fact that you don't know it is part of his strategy! Any influence he has over you has been given to him by you.

Under whose sovereignty will you function? Are you still a child of Satan, moved about at his will? Jesus spoke of the Pharisees as children of the devil, because they were motivated by his will; they were under his control. When a person is born again, he is taken out of the kingdom of darkness and becomes a citizen of the kingdom of God. The word of God delivers people from the power of Satan. The great hymn of the church, "A Mighty Fortress," says in the third stanza,

> And tho' this world, with devils filled,
> Should threaten to undo us;

> We will not fear, for God has willed
> His truth to triumph through us:
> The prince of darkness grim,
> We tremble not for him;
> His rage we can endure,
> For lo! his doom is sure,
> One little word shall fell him.

What is that word? It is found in the second stanza.

> Christ Jesus it is He;
> Lord Sabaoth his
>   Name,
> From age to age the
>   same

And, the hymn concludes,

> His kingdom is forever.

God has already shown His commitment to us. The solution to the thirst we experience for commitment to absolutes is found in only one place. There is only one absolute—Jesus Christ, the absolute Ruler of the universe, the Alpha and the Omega, the Beginning and the End.

PRAYER

Almighty God, whom truly to know is everlasting life: Grant us so perfectly to know your Son Jesus Christ to be the way, the truth, and the life, that we may steadfastly follow his steps in the way that leads to eternal life; through Jesus Christ your Son our Lord, who lives and reigns with you, in the unity of the Holy Spirit, one God, for ever and ever. Amen.
> —Collect for the Fifth Sunday of Easter

— QUESTIONS —

Do you believe Satan exists?

What trials are you experiencing right now?

What victories have you known in Christ recently?

CHAPTER 17

Thirsting for Communion

I speak as to wise men; judge for yourselves what I say. The cup of blessing which we bless, is it not the communion of the blood of Christ? The bread which we break, is it not the communion of the body of Christ? For we, though many, are one bread and one body; for we all partake of that one bread (1 Cor. 10:15-17).

For I received from the Lord that which I also delivered to you: that the Lord Jesus on the same night in which He was betrayed took bread; and when He had given thanks, He broke it and said, 'Take, eat; this is My body which is broken for you; do this in remembrance of Me." In the same manner He also took the cup after supper, saying, "This cup is the new covenant in My blood. This do, as often as you drink it, in remembrance of Me." For as often as you eat this bread and drink this cup, you proclaim the Lord's death till He comes (1 Cor. 11:23-26).

THESE ARE FAMILIAR WORDS from Saint Paul concerning various aspects of the Eucharist, or the celebration of Holy Communion. Paul, of course, was not present in the Upper Room on the night of the Last Supper; in fact, he did not become a Christian until at least three years after the Ascension. Still, Paul's account of the Eucharist is the oldest we have. All of Paul's letters were written before the Gospels and the Acts were written. As the oldest account of the events of the Last Supper, this is the one that has been established in the mind of the church right from the beginning.

The Lord's Supper, or Holy Eucharist, has been the central act of worship in the Christian church right from the days of the apostles. We participate in this service so often that we can come to take it for granted. We are creatures of habit, and we can very quickly fall into routine patterns of behavior and action. Sometimes we cease to think of what we are doing and it becomes merely a ritualistic performance. The Eucharist is not intended to be that way. It is intended to be the means by which believers in Jesus Christ can experience His presence with them and can know the fulfillment of their thirst for communion with God here and now.

The clearest expression of the church as a body of believers is found in Holy Communion. There we thank God for the basis of all our fellowship, the Cross of Christ. We rejoice that in the Cross, all human barriers have been broken down—we are all alike, sinners in need of saving grace. When we eat of the same bread and drink of the same cup (not literally, but symbolically), we acknowledge that we are indeed brothers and sisters, and together we celebrate the guarantee of our eternal relationships with God and one another. We recognize that no one can separate us for all eternity. We share His peace and love with one another. We are strengthened to serve Him in the world. And in one another, we perceive the body of Christ, each with a call and a function to perform to make His life real in the world.

Three Views

Traditionally, there have been three ways of understanding the significance of this sacred meal. The first we might consider the reformed view. Calvin and other reformed theologians hold that Christ's body is in heaven, having ascended to the Father, and therefore is not present in the elements used. Christ meets His people at the Communion table not by bodily presence in the elements, but by the presence of the Holy Spirit within the heart of the believer. The reformed view is that the Lord's Supper is a memorial feast. The bread and the wine are merely bread and wine and one could use milk and cookies just as well, because there is no particular symbolism in the elements. The idea is that at the feast, you remember what Christ has done. The significance is found in the phrase "do this in remembrance of Me." It's looking backward to Christ's finished work upon the Cross that obtained our salvation. Communion is referred to as an "ordinance" in this tradition. The word *ordinance* means "law." We talk about a community ordinance or a state ordinance; to this tradition, the Communion celebration is done because Jesus told us to do it. In the churches that hold to this view, the Communion is usually given four times a year or on the first Sunday of each month.

The orthodox view is held by orthodox churches, the Roman tradition, and some Lutheran and Anglican churches. It holds that at that moment when the priest utters the words of consecration, the bread and the wine are changed into the body and blood of Christ by a supernatural act of God. The term used is "transsubstantiation," which means that the substance of the elements is changed.

This view is based on a complicated philosophical system of Aristotle, that all that exists can be explained in terms of its basic substance and then what he called its "accidence." Accidence is the external appearance of something; the substance is its basic nature.

Accidence can change, disappear, or be added, while the basic substance remains the same. Accidence neither constitutes essence nor flows from it. Substance, on the other hand, is what we understand as the primary being of things. In this connection, the orthodox theologian would say that the accidence of the bread and wine—the way they look, the way they taste, and so forth—remains unchanged. Only the substance actually changes, by a mystical operation of the power of God. From the moment those words are spoken, the bread and wine are no longer bread and wine, even though they look that way to the eye of flesh; they have become the body and the blood of Christ.

In the middle there is a third view, that the bread and wine are forever bread and wine and nothing else. They do not change into anything, but because Jesus said "This is My Body; this is My Blood," when we receive them in faith we are spiritually receiving Christ's life into our own. This would be the work of the Holy Spirit present in the consecration and in the believer. This view holds that Christ is not literally present in the bread and the wine as the orthodox would say, but He is spiritually present there. It is based on the thought that the disciples, on the night of the Last Supper, would not have imagined Jesus to mean that the bread and the cup were His body, and blood in a literal sense, but that in some mystical sense He was taking the elements of bread and wine and saying that they represented His body and His blood.

Both this view and the orthodox view understand the action of the Holy Spirit to be present and necessary, so they would refer to the eucharistic celebration as a sacrament, rather than an ordinance. In these churches, the Eucharist is celebrated at most services of worship, often several times during the week.

Regardless of human tradition, some things are common to our understanding of the meaning of Holy Communion.

Past, Present, and Future

In order to get a full view of the significance of the Eucharist, we have to note that it looks in three directions in terms of time. It looks backward: Jesus clearly said, "Do this in remembrance of me." As you receive the Lord's Supper, you are to remember what He did on your behalf. Thus, Paul says in 1 Corinthians 11:26: ". . . as often as you eat this bread and drink this cup, you proclaim the Lord's death till He comes." It looks at the present, in that we are to be spiritually nourished by the receiving of the Eucharist. And it looks to the future, "till He comes."

The Eucharist is a continual reenactment of the sacrifice of Christ upon the cross. It is not a sacrifice, but a remembrance of the sacrifice; we are not offering a new sacrifice to the Lord in atonement for sin. Jesus has already done that on the cross, once for all people, for all time. The Eucharist is a sacrifice for us, but it is a sacrifice of praise and thanksgiving. We offer to the Lord the very word thanksgiving: the word *Eucharist* is a Greek word that means "thanksgiving." So when we talk about observing or celebrating the Eucharist, we are celebrating a thanksgiving service for what God has done for us in the past. It is a commemoration of Christ's death, for which we give God praise and thanksgiving. During the Eucharist, when we look back and remember, we fix our attention on our redemption.

But we also need to remember, as we receive the Eucharist, that the Lord is constantly active in our lives: He is constantly providing for our needs. Communion with the Lord is here and now. The basis for this understanding comes from a number of Scriptures.

In John 6 we find the story of the feeding of the multitudes with loaves and fishes. The passage tells of the effect of that great miracle upon the people. "Then those men, when they had seen the sign that Jesus did, said, 'This is truly the Prophet who is to come into the world.' Therefore when Jesus perceived that they were about to come and take Him by force to make Him king, He departed again to a mountain by Himself alone" (John 6:14–15).

In their excitement at the miraculous provision, the people remembered the words of Moses: "The LORD your God will raise up for you a Prophet like me from your midst, from your brethren. Him you shall hear" (Deut. 18:15). They remembered that prophecy because they were reminded that under Moses, God's people were provided with manna and water in the wilderness. Jesus was perceived as a prophet like unto Moses, providing in this miraculous way for their needs.

Can you imagine what the five thousand people said to their neighbors who were not there when they went home that night? The figure of five thousand counts only men—no one knows how many women and children were there. The reaction would have been something close to pandemonium. The next day, people from everywhere came to find Jesus.

Verse 25: "And when they found Him on the other side of the sea, they said to Him, 'Rabbi, when did You come here?' Jesus answered them and said, 'Most assuredly, I say to you, you seek Me, not because you saw the signs, but because you ate of the loaves and were filled.' "

Jesus was not impressed by the fact that multitudes sought Him out the next day, because He could clearly see that the reason they sought Him out was because He had filled their bellies. He was a kind of meal ticket—it would be very convenient to have Him around! Jesus knew that this was in the back of their minds. So He used this occasion to teach something very profound and very important, which I want you to consider in terms of Communion.

Verse 27: "Do not labor for the food which perishes, but for the food which endures to everlasting life, which the Son of Man will give you, because God the Father has set His seal on Him."

Jesus tells them that the food they are seeking, the bread and fish they ate, is perishable food. But the food that He, the Son of God, will give them will endure. What did He mean by that?

> Therefore they said to Him, "What sign will You perform then, that we may see it and believe You? What work will You do? Our fathers ate the manna in the desert; as it is written, 'He gave them bread from heaven to eat.' " Then Jesus said to them, "Most assuredly, I say to you, Moses did not give you the bread from heaven, but My Father gives you the true bread from heaven. For the bread of God is He who comes down from heaven and gives life to the world." Then they said to Him, "Lord, give us this bread always" (vv. 30–34).

Jesus is saying that what happened to the people of God under the old covenant, when God supplied the manna, was an earthly picture of what He Himself had done when He came down from heaven as the bread that God supplied. So they said to Him, "Lord, give us this bread always."

Verse 35: "And Jesus said to them, 'I am the bread of life. He who comes to Me shall never hunger, and he who believes in Me shall never thirst.' " Jesus is making an astounding claim. He is saying that the basic hunger and thirst in the heart of man is such that no earthly food can ever satisfy. It can be satisfied in Him alone. He was saying, "I am the bread of heaven, specially designed to meet your inner needs."

But I said to you that you have seen Me and yet do not believe. All that the Father gives Me will come to Me, and the one who comes to Me I will by no means cast out. For I have come down from heaven, not to do My own will, but the will of Him who sent Me. This is the will of the Father who sent Me, . . . that everyone who sees the Son, and believes in Him may have everlasting life; and I will raise him up at the last day (vv. 36–40).

Later in the chapter, Jesus is still teaching, and says:

Most assuredly, I say to you, he who believes in Me has everlasting life. I am the bread of life. Your fathers ate the manna in the wilderness, and are dead. This is the bread which comes down from heaven, that one may eat of it and not die. I am the living bread which came down from heaven. If anyone eats of this bread, he will live forever; and the bread that I shall give is My flesh, which I shall give for the life of the world (vv. 47–51).

Jesus said, "I have come down from heaven as the bread upon which you must feed. And what is that bread? It is my flesh which I will offer up for the salvation of the world." The people didn't understand those words. They made the same mistake that was made again and again when people listened to Jesus' teaching. They took what Jesus said in a literal fashion. "The Jews therefore quarreled among themselves, saying, 'How can this Man give us His flesh to eat?' " (v. 52).

How can this man give us his flesh to eat? What does he think we are, cannibals? Jesus' reply is interesting. He didn't challenge their literal interpretation. "Most assuredly, I say to you, unless you eat the flesh of the Son of Man and drink His blood, you have no life in you. Whoever eats My flesh and drinks My blood has eternal life, and I will raise him up at the last day" (vv. 53–54).

Jesus is giving some very hard teaching. He is saying you MUST eat His flesh and drink His blood or else you will not have life within you. He doesn't explain what it means to eat His flesh and drink His blood, only that it is something God has provided for the salvation of the world, and without it no one will see the kingdom of God.

Verses 55–56: "For My flesh is food indeed, and My blood is drink indeed. He who eats My flesh and drinks My blood abides in Me, and I in him." Can you imagine how this sounded? Religious Jewish people were not allowed to drink the blood of any animal. One aspect of kosher cooking and of killing an animal in a kosher way is that all the blood is drained off. The Jewish law did not allow the consumption of any blood, and yet here is Jesus saying, "You must drink my blood. You must eat my flesh," and without explanation.

"As the living Father sent Me, and I live because of the Father, so he who feeds on Me will live because of Me. This is the bread which came down from heaven—not as your fathers ate the manna, and are dead. He who eats this bread will live forever" (vv. 57–58).

Notice the reaction of the people. Verse 60: "Therefore many of His disciples, when they heard this, said, 'This is a hard saying; who can understand it?' " And verse 66: "From that time many of His disciples went back and walked with Him no more." This is the first evidence of people turning away from the Lord. Up to this point it looked as though everyone would believe in Him and accept Him. He had great crowds everywhere He went. He taught and people were greatly excited about His ministry. Now comes the turning point.

The teaching of Jesus as the bread of life was offensive then, and still is now, because He was very clearly saying, "Without Me you cannot live. Unless you come to Me, you have no life in you. Unless you drink My blood and eat My flesh you shall not live forever."

That teaching was in the back of the disciples' minds on that night when He took bread and said, "This is My body which is broken for you; do this in remembrance of Me," and when He took a cup of wine and said, "This cup is the new covenant in My blood. This do, as often as you drink it, in remembrance of Me" (1 Cor. 11:24–25).

What the Scripture leads us to understand is that the bread and the wine of the Communion feast have some means of supplying for us the body without which Jesus said we cannot live. That wine is His blood, in a mystic and spiritual sense, without which we shall not find life. When the elements are received in faith, we receive the body and blood of Christ in some mystic and spiritual sense and we are spiritually nourished by Him. That is an important part of our spiritual life; it is a means of grace, whereby we grow.

Background in Jewish Worship

To the vast majority of Christians since the days of the apostles, the Eucharist has been and remains the central service of Christian worship. It is recorded in the book of Acts, that for the first years after the ascension of Christ, believers continued worshiping in the temple and the synagogue on Saturday. And on the first day of the week they met in homes—because there were no churches—for the Lord's Supper, or the Lord's Service. The synagogue service, to which Jesus and all the apostles were accustomed in those days—and it is very much the same today—consisted of these elements: a lesson from the Law, a lesson from the Prophets, the singing and recitation of Psalms, prayers, a sermon, and an offering. Those six elements continued in the worship service of early believers in Christ. They met in homes around the Lord's Table, to remember His death and to feed daily upon Him, as they received the sacrament in faith.

By the year A.D. 70, when it became very clear that Christianity and Judaism were not the same thing, and that Christianity was not merely a sect of the Jews, the synagogue and the church separated. The two services came together, and the Jewish synagogue service was linked with the Lord's Supper into the service you and I know as Holy Communion. It is essentially the same in structure today as it has been since the days of the apostles.

Holy Communion looks backward to what Christ accomplished on the Cross, and looks to the present in that every time you come to the altar in faith you are actually nourished spiritually. You may say to yourself, "I don't feel it." Well, do you feel significantly enhanced, physically, after you eat a meal? Doesn't it take a while for the food you have consumed to become part of your very flesh and bone? How any meal of roast beef and potatoes becomes skin, blood, muscle, and tissue is a mystery to me! But I know that I must eat food to survive. How the Eucharist—the receiving of a tiny sip of wine or grape juice and a thin wafer or small piece of bread—ministers spiritual grace, is likewise a mystery. But I do know that it is important to my spiritual survival.

Looking Forward

There is a third aspect to Communion. To understand the Eucharist in its full significance we must also look forward. We are to do this, Paul says, "till He comes again."

The New Testament speaks of the church as the bride of Christ.

God, through the Holy Spirit, is calling out of the world a bride and preparing that bride to be united forever with Christ. Christ is the Bridegroom and we are the bride.

> And the twenty-four elders and the four living creatures fell down and worshiped God who sat on the throne, saying "Amen! Alleluia!" Then a voice came from the throne, saying, "Praise our God, all you His servants and those who fear Him, both small and great!" And I heard, as it were, the voice of a great multitude, as the sound of many waters and as the sound of mighty thunderings, saying "Alleluia! For the Lord God Omnipotent reigns! Let us be glad and rejoice and give Him glory, for the marriage of the Lamb has come, and His wife has made herself ready." And to her it was granted to be arrayed in fine linen, clean and bright, for the fine linen is the righteous acts of the saints (Rev. 19:4–8).

This passage describes the marriage supper of the Lamb. One significant element of Holy Communion, as you come week after week to be fed from the table of the Lord, is the anticipation of the day when we shall be permanently and forever united with Christ. That is spoken of as a marriage, the great marriage supper of the Lamb. Remember that Jesus said to the twelve disciples at the Last Supper, "I will no longer drink of the fruit of the vine until that day when I drink it new in the kingdom of God" (Mark 14:25). In the meantime, you and I are gathering around His table in anticipation of the day when we shall partake of the marriage supper of the Lamb and shall forever be with Him.

Participating fully in the Holy Communion is the means of satisfying our thirst for communion with God. It involves looking backward, to the moment of redemption, and forward to the time when we are permanently and forever united with Christ. And in the meantime it is means of feeding upon His body and blood, without which He said we shall not have eternal life. It is recognizing the body of Christ in the believers around us, and preparing to share eternity with them.

PRAYER

Gracious Father, whose blessed Son Jesus Christ came down from heaven to be the true bread which gives life to the world: Evermore give us this bread, that he may live in us, and we in him; who lives and reigns with you and the Holy Spirit, one God, now and for ever. Amen.
—Collect for the Fourth Sunday in Lent

— QUESTIONS —

How often do you receive communion?

Do you sense the Lord's presence in the sacrament?

Do you sense the Lord's presence in the believers around you?

Do you sense the Lord's presence with you?

CHAPTER 18

Thirsting for Destiny

IN 1988, AROUND THE FEAST of Yom Kippur, the Lord Jesus Christ was supposed to come again. Someone had figured out that this was the date and written a book. Great numbers of sincere Christians believed it. Some sold their businesses; some quit their jobs in order to pray and fast and be with their families. Most paid no attention whatsoever, except to laugh at the news briefs on the topic.

Well, the day came and the day passed. The media made quite a joke out of it, as they do any time that there is a stir from a group or a religion claiming to have inside knowledge about the end of the world. There have been so many false starts that the world has almost convinced itself it isn't going to happen. And yet, whenever there is a prediction that Jesus is coming, the world holds its breath. There is in us a sense that someday time will stop; someday God will reveal His glory. Our souls thirst for this destiny.

The whole matter of the second coming of Jesus is raised in a question found in Peter's second letter: "Where is the promise of His coming?"

Peter advises those "who have obtained like precious faith with us by the righteousness of our God and Savior Jesus Christ" (2 Peter 1:1). That description would apply to us, as well. He wants us to be mindful of the words spoken by the prophets about Jesus, and the apostles: "knowing this first: that scoffers will come in the last days, walking according to their own lusts, and saying, 'Where is the promise of His coming? For since the fathers fell asleep, all things continue as they were from the beginning of creation' " (2:3–4).

The question is asked in a context of doubt and skepticism. Not only will there be scoffers in the last days, but there will be people following their own passions, who have set them as the dominating course of their lives, without reference to the will of God, or right or wrong. People will say, "Nothing's changed about mankind." This will be a characteristic of the day in which this question will be raised as a joke—"So, when's He coming?"

In order to find our destiny, we need to step away from doubt and derision and look seriously at what the Bible has to say about the second coming of Jesus Christ. Is belief in the Second Coming an essential aspect of the Christian faith? What does the Bible say about it? Does belief in the Second Coming have any practical consequences for the believer?

Essential Belief

The second coming of Christ is mentioned far more in Scripture than is His first appearance. The Old Testament contains so many references to His coming as King and in great power, that when He came in humility, the Jewish people for whom He came did not even recognize Him. Part of the problem was the blindness of their hearts due to unbelief, but the other part was the great number of references to the fact that this promised One was going to come as a powerful king. From the vantage point of Christendom, we are able to separate His first coming in humility from His Second Coming in great power and glory. But this distinction was not clear to the people of Jesus' day. In the New Testament, the second coming of Christ is mentioned in practically every book. In some places, it is given extended treatment. In fact, the Bible ends with the reference to His coming: "Even so, come, Lord Jesus!"

With so much material concerning the subject, we can see that belief in the Second Coming is essential for Christians. The second line of evidence is in terms of the history of the church and our faith. It is part of both ancient creeds of our church. The Apostles' Creed comes from the seventh century, but in its early formation goes back to the days of the apostles themselves. When the apostles were baptizing new converts into the faith, they had a list of things in which the new converts professed to believe. That list has become the basis for what we know as the Apostles' Creed. It included the phrase, "He will come again to judge the living and the dead." In the Nicene Creed, which is used in services of Holy Communion, we say, "He will come again in glory to judge the living and the dead." Both creeds, used throughout Christendom for centuries, have as a central aspect the belief in the second coming of Christ.

Biblical Witness

Scripture gives much detail about the event itself. What does it say about the conditions of the world at the time of His coming?

> But know this, that in the last days perilous times will come: For men will be lovers of themselves, lovers of money, boasters, proud, blasphemers, disobedient to parents, unthankful, unholy, unloving, unforgiving, slanderers, without self-control, brutal, despisers of good, traitors, headstrong, haughty, lovers of pleasure rather than lovers of God, having a form of godliness but denying its power. And from such people turn away! (2 Tim. 3:1–5).

This description makes chills pass up and down your spine, doesn't it? This is the general attitude of the last days. There is nothing in the Bible of the surface optimism that is often promoted in churches— that in every day in every way, the human race is getting better and better. Scripture makes it very clear that as we progress to the end of the age, things will get worse. Actually, that list of sins has been present since the law was given to make people aware of them. They have always been part of our unregenerate nature. What will distinguish the last days, however, is that the sins will not be hidden, as if they were something to be ashamed of, but displayed in public, without repentance or shame, "for their folly will be manifest to all" (v. 9*b*).

Notice, however, that it will not be a time without religion. Religion will flourish in that kind of environment. Churches will be operating right up to the end. They will conduct their services, but the reality of worship—the power of the presence of God—will be denied. Worship will become empty, ritualistic form. Bible studies will continue, with people "always learning and never able to come to the knowledge of the truth" (v. 7). They won't come to a knowledge of the truth because they resist it.

All those things are already manifested to an alarming degree in the world in which we live. It is certainly descriptive of our days to say that there are lovers of money, for instance. The stock market scams prove that. Many children are suing their parents because they disagree with them. The rampant reports of child abuse and spouse and parent abuse give testimony to unloving, unforgiving, brutal people without self-control. The spread of pornography and the increase of sexual explicitness in all entertainment media indicate that there are great numbers who love pleasure rather than God.

And in the churches, sadly, many hold to the form of religion and deny the power of God. In fact, these persons become very angry when anyone raises the matter of a faith that actually makes a difference. A man said to me not long ago, "I want a church that won't make a claim on me." I replied, "That won't be hard to find." There are people who want churches to make them comfortable with what they are doing; they don't want to hear a message that will transform their lives. This is another characteristic of the last days. The basic teachings of Christianity will be challenged—in fact, the scoffers of whom Peter speaks will be primarily within the church! The doctrines of the faith have already come under question—the Resurrection, the Incarnation, the Virgin Birth have all begun to be relegated to places of unimportance. And, being set aside, they begin to perish from people's minds. Peter refers to this forgetfulness:

> For this they willfully forget: that by the word of God the heavens were of old, and the earth standing out of the water and in the water, by which the world that then existed perished, being flooded with water. But the heavens and the earth which now exist are kept in store by the same word, reserved for fire until the day of judgment and perdition of ungodly men (2 Pet. 3:5–7).

When?

The gospel of Matthew contains another description of the world in the last days prior to the coming of the Lord. The situation describes a conversation between Jesus and His disciples, perhaps after they had worshiped together in the temple at Jerusalem. They may have walked out through the Lion Gate across to the Mount of Olives, and looked back at the beauty of the Temple, gleaming in the sunlight. "His disciples came up to show Him the buildings of the temple. And Jesus said to them, 'Do you not see all these things? Assuredly, I say to you, not one stone shall be left here upon another, that shall not be thrown down'" (Matt. 24:1*b*, 2).

The destruction of the temple they were discussing occurred in the year A.D. 70. Some who heard Jesus say these words no doubt witnessed the destruction of the temple. These words were literally fulfilled. The disciples came to Jesus and asked Him, "When will these things be?" And then, a more important question: "And what will be the sign of Your coming, and of the end of the age?" (v. 3).

The rest of the chapter contains Jesus' words in response to the question about the end of the age.

> And Jesus answered and said to them, "Take heed that no one deceives you. For many will come in My name, saying, 'I am the Christ,' and will deceive many. And you will hear of wars and rumors of wars. See that you are not troubled; for all these things must come to pass, but the end is not yet. For nation will rise against nation, and kingdom against kingdom. And there will be famines, pestilences, and earthquakes in various places. All these are the beginning of sorrows" (vv. 4–8).

Before Jesus comes, you can expect wars, famines, pestilences, and earthquakes. These have continued throughout history. But think of Jesus' words about kingdom against kingdom in light of the spiritual battles that are being waged as well, because He makes it clear that there will be a time of intense persecution for the believing Christian.

> Then they will deliver you up to tribulation and kill you, and you will be hated by all nations for My name's sake. And then many will be offended, will betray one another, and will hate one another. Then many false prophets will rise up and deceive many. And because lawlessness will abound, the love of many will grow cold (vv. 9–12).

Jesus is saying that the church will not be very successful in converting the world to Christ. The age will get darker and darker, but God will work in the true believer and in the church. The true church of Jesus Christ will get brighter and brighter by comparison; but as that happens, the anger of the world against Christ and His followers will increase, until they seek to put those who trust in Him to death.

We have seen examples of that attitude in this century. During World War II, Dietrich Bonhoeffer and other Christians were put to death by the Nazis. In Africa and South America, many Christians have died at the hands of violent political regimes. Jesus had words of comfort for those people: "But he who endures to the end shall be saved" (v. 13).

The conditions of the world have been ready for Christ to come since the days He walked the earth, but there are other factors to consider. Bear in mind that Jesus Himself said that "of that day and hour no one knows, not even the angels of heaven, but My Father only" (v. 36). Yet Jesus gave other indications of when He would come.

"And this gospel of the kingdom will be preached in all the world as a witness to all the nations, and then the end will come" (v. 14). The means to do this has only recently been possible! The various languages of the world have been explored and there are groups translating the gospel into thousands of dialects even as you read this. Technology is being developed that would enable Christian radio broadcasts to the utmost parts of the earth. And in every denomination around the world, the decade that begins in 1990 is seen as a time of evangelism in preparation for the Lord's return.

Jesus said that although there will be false signs and false Christs, those who are alert will not be caught by surprise. "Now learn this parable from the fig tree: When its branch has already become tender and puts forth leaves, you know that summer is near. So you also, when you see all these things, know that it is near—at the doors!" (vv. 32–33). That is a word to believers—keep alert! Life will go on seemingly as usual: "For as in the days before the flood, they were eating and drinking, marrying and giving in marriage, until the day that Noah entered the ark, and did not know until the flood came and took them all away, so also will the coming of the Son of Man be" (vv. 38–39).

Paul echoes these words in his letter to the church at Thessalonica:

For you yourselves know perfectly that the day of the Lord so comes as a thief in the night. For when they say, "Peace and safety!" then sudden destruction comes upon them, as labor pains upon a pregnant woman. And they shall not escape. But you, brethren, are not in darkness, so that this Day should overtake you as a thief. You are all sons of light and sons of the day. We are not of the night nor of darkness. Therefore let us not sleep, as others do, but let us watch and be sober (1 Thess. 5:2–6).

Cosmic Event

Jesus describes His second coming as a cosmic event. It will be something that no one can miss!

> Immediately after the tribulation of those days the sun will be darkened, and the moon will not give its light; the stars will fall from heaven, and the powers of the heavens will be shaken. Then the sign of the Son of Man will appear in heaven, and then all the tribes of the earth will mourn, and they will see the Son of Man coming on the clouds of heaven with power and great glory. And He will send His angels with a great sound of a trumpet, and they will gather together His elect from the four winds, from one end of heaven to the other (Matt. 24:29–31).

It will be the noisiest event in history! The trumpet of God will sound; the angels will shout, just so that no one fails to notice. His first Advent was quiet and subdued; just a few shepherds heard the angels. The second coming of Jesus will be something the entire earth will know. "But the day of the Lord will come as a thief in the night, in which the heavens will pass away with a great noise, and the elements will melt with fervent heat; both the earth and the works that are in it will be burned up" (2 Peter 3:10).

Peter also uses the idea of the coming of the Lord like a thief in the night. His description makes it clear that the Second Coming of Christ is the end of human history as we know it, the end of the elements of earth.

The Eternal Kingdom

Many things are said to occur at the Second Coming. One is the resurrection of the dead. Jesus said:

> Most assuredly, I say to you, the hour is coming, and now is, when the dead will hear the voice of the Son of God; and those who hear will live. For as the Father has life in Himself, so He has granted the Son to have life in Himself, and has given Him authority to execute judgment also, because He is the Son of Man. Do not marvel at this; for the hour is coming in which all who are in the graves will hear His voice and come forth—those who have done good, to the resurrection of life, and those who have done evil, to the resurrection of condemnation (John 5:25–29).

Another part of the Second Coming is the judgment of all the living and the dead. "For we all must appear before the judgment seat of Christ, that each one may receive the things done in the body, according to what he has done, whether good or bad" (2 Cor. 5:10).

Yet another aspect is the establishment of the eternal kingdom. You may be thinking as you've been reading along, "If it's true that things will get worse and worse, where is the kingdom of peace that Scripture talks about? Where is Jesus' reign of peace?"

We need to remember Jesus' words that His kingdom was not of this world. The prophet Isaiah tells us that the throne of the Messiah is eternal, without end. Jesus' kingdom is not, never has been, nor shall it ever be, an earthly kingdom. There were Jews in His day who did not understand that, and there have been believers ever since who don't. The last question Scripture records the disciples asking Jesus before His Ascension was: "Master, will You at this time [His second coming] return the kingdom to Israel?" (Acts 1:6). If I were Jesus, I would have given up on them. I would have thought, "Here I've been with you for three and a half years, and you still don't understand! You still think I'm talking about an earthly rule, sitting on a throne made by human hands."

Peter makes it clear that this is not the case. We are not dealing with this old, tired, earth. "Nevertheless we, according to His promise, look for new heavens and a new earth in which righteousness dwells" (2 Pet. 3:13).

Revelation 21 also speaks of a new heaven and a new earth. "Now I saw a new heaven and a new earth, for the first heaven and the first earth had passed away. Also there was no more sea" (v. 1). Then John describes the New Jerusalem, coming down out of heaven from God, prepared as a bride adorned for her husband.

And I heard a loud voice from heaven saying, "Behold, the tabernacle of God is with men, and He will dwell with them, and they shall be His people. God Himself will be with them and be their God. And God will wipe away every tear from their eyes; there shall be no more death, nor sorrow, nor crying. There shall be no more pain, for the former things have passed away. Then He who sat on the throne said, "Behold, I make all things new" (vv. 3–5*a*).

"Peace on earth, good will to men" will never be fulfilled in this life. This doesn't mean we are not to work for peace, to try to extend it as far as we can. Rather, we are to realize that the answer to peace is not within our power. Ultimately, peace comes about with the transformation of our hearts when God Himself takes away the hostility, the hatred, and the frustration that finds its way so easily into them.

Practical Consequences

If the world hasn't changed much, and no one knows the time of the Second Coming except the Father, what are the practical considerations for believers? Peter deals with this question as a continuation of his statement that the world will be consumed. "Therefore, since all these things will be dissolved, what manner of persons ought you to be in holy conduct and godliness?" (2 Pet. 3:11).

We are creatures of time who live our lives in eternity. Even though our days are limited, because of our belief in Christ we live them in reference to eternity. What kind of lives would be lived in holy conduct and godliness?

Paul wrote to Titus:

> For the grace of God that brings salvation has appeared to all men, teaching us that, denying ungodliness and worldly lusts, we should live soberly, righteously, and godly in the present age, looking for the blessed hope and glorious appearing of our great God and Savior Jesus Christ, who gave Himself for us, that He might redeem us from every lawless deed and purify for Himself His own special people, zealous for good works (Titus 2:11–14).

What kind of good works? Paul goes on to give a long list. Believers are to be subject to rulers and authorities—obedient to the laws to which we are subject (3:1). When, for instance, was the last time you drove over the legal speed limit?

We are also instructed to speak evil of no one (v. 2*a*). The tongue is always in need of purifying by the Holy Spirit. This purification will go a long way toward helping us "be peaceable, gentle, showing all humility to all men" (v. 2*b*). Pride has no place in holy conduct.

Paul also suggests that we "avoid foolish disputes, genealogies, contentions, and strivings about the law; for they are unprofitable and useless" (v. 9). There are better things for us to do with our time if we are to live in godliness. There are "urgent needs" to be met (v. 14).

Certainly Jesus spoke of that urgency in the parable of the sheep and the goats.

> When the Son of Man comes in His glory, and all the holy angels with Him, then He will sit on the throne of His glory. All the nations will be gathered before Him, and He will separate them one from another, as a shepherd divides his sheep from the goats. And He will set the sheep on His right hand, but the goats on the left. Then the King will say to those on His right hand, "Come, you

blessed of My Father, inherit the kingdom prepared for you from the foundation of the world: for I was hungry and you gave Me food; I was thirsty and you gave Me drink; I was a stranger and you took Me in; I was naked and you clothed Me; I was sick and you visited Me; I was in prison and you came to Me" (Matt. 25:31–36).

The life we are given to live is a life with a destiny. We are given days to live now to the praise of His glory. This is the day of salvation. This is the moment we choose. This is how we lay up our treasures in heaven.

Jesus is coming. Don't let the skeptics take your attention away from living a life of godliness. Moment by moment, live the words of destiny that end Scripture: Come, Lord Jesus!

___ PRAYER ___

O God, whose blessed Son came into the world that he might destroy the works of the devil and make us children of God and heirs of eternal life: Grant that, having this hope, we may purify ourselves as he is pure; that when he comes again with power and great glory, we may be made like him in his eternal and glorious kingdom; where he lives and reigns with you and the Holy Spirit, one God, for ever and ever. Amen.

—Proper 27

— QUESTIONS —

What signs of the last days do you see around you?

Are there acts of righteousness that you have been avoiding?

How would your life be different if you knew that Jesus was coming soon?